BLATHER

A LOAD OF BLATHER

Unreal reports from Ireland & Beyond

Dave Walsh
Barry Kavanagh
Damien DeBarra

NONSUCH

First published 2008

Nonsuch Publishing
73 Lower Leeson Street,
Dublin 2, Ireland
www.nonsuchireland.com

British Library Cataloguing in Publication Data.
A catalogue record for this book is available from the British Library.

ISBN 978 1 84588 922 7

Typesetting and origination by The History Press Ltd.
Printed in Ireland, by Betaprint

CONTENTS

ACKNOWLEDGEMENTS

Everybody that's contributed in some way to keeping Blather.net running over the years, especially Barry Kavanagh, Damien DeBarra and my sister Sue Walsh. Gerry McGovern for making me do it. Stephen and Aidan McCarron at Hosting 365 for the web hosting. Ronan Gahan, Paul Clerkin and Mick Cunningham for the all the help, advice and abuse. Ronan Colgan at Nonsuch for convincing me that this book could be done. The late Robert Anton Wilson for being a fan of Blather.net before I knew that he knew I even existed. Our families and girlfriends and boyfriends and wives for putting up with us. Everyone who's supplied content or posted a comment or hurled obscenities at us over the years. You know you are. We love you too.

Dave Walsh

INTRODUCTION:
BLATHER DOESN'T CARE

By the time you read this our little website, Blather.net, will be eleven years old. That's eleven years of spouting opinionated rants on everything from lake monsters to lepreporn, from clitorises to mystery cannonballs.

It all began back in May 1997. I was at my desk in a trendy loft-space, just off Westland Row in Dublin. Gerry McGovern, one of the bosses at the upstart internet startup company Nua, approached me, somewhat tentatively, and suggested that I start writing an internet newsletter on weird stuff. He knew I was into UFOs, the paranormal and that class of thing.

I wracked my brain for a name. When I came up with the name *Blather* it felt like cheating: it was outright theft from a short-lived journal back in the 1930s run (into the ground) by a young man later to be known as Flann O'Brien. The original *Blather*'s manifesto read:

> As we advance to make our bow, you will search in vain for signs of servility or for any evidence of a desire to please. We are an arrogant and depraved body of men. We are as proud as bantams and as vain as peacocks.
> "Blather doesn't care." A sardonic laugh escapes us as we bow, cruel and cynical hounds that we are. It is a terrible laugh, the laugh of lost men. Do you get the smell of porter?
> (*Blather*, issue 1, 1934)

It didn't take long for the modern *Blather* to become as depraved as its predecessor.

On 12 May 1997, the first issue of this *Blather* went up online, and was soon producing articles about lactating men, a trawler being sunk by a cow that fell from the sky, cloning, euthanasia, rains of toads, kidney theft, moving statues, cryptozoology and Bram Stoker. Within a couple of years, I had written about UFO sightings in Cork, hung out on Dublin beaches in mid-December with UFO spotters, looked for monsters in lakes, pretty much joined the Hellfire Club, and had been branded a Satanist and a pornographer.

It was too good to last. I left Nua, and wasn't paid to do *Blather* anymore. It lost focus. I got fed up with paranormal stories, so I enlisted the help of Barry Kavanagh, who interviewed comic legend Alan Moore for the site, and Damien De Barra, who turned up out of the blue with an archaeological article entitled 'What Did the Romans Ever Do for Us?' In the following years, the site slowly moved from being an albatross around my neck to becoming the properly-functioning multi-blog website Blather.net, with fancy things like databases.

But we never went big. Back in the bad old days of dot com nonsense, everybody was selling their websites to business to make the 'big money'. There was talk about Blather.net getting investment so that we could be paid to work from Blather High Command – and it stayed talk.

We never wanted it to be work. We have fun, some of it completely puerile, some of it quite serious. We've wandered away from the paranormal stuff a bit, and started obsessing over mythology, folklore, archaeology, photography, music… well, anything that catches our fancy. I've always said to Blather.net writers: 'I don't care what it's about, just make it interesting.'

The chapters in this book are really just the scum off the top of the hundreds of articles on Blather.net, and we've chosen some fairly daft stuff. Enjoy – but remember, if you don't like this book, send it back to us. It's not that we'll refund the money or anything, but if we get back an unwanted copy in perfect nick, then we can sell it again and make twice the cash.

Do you get the smell of porter?

Dave Walsh

X-Files if you want, but perhaps that too was part of the zeitgeist, in some sort of pre-millennial tension that spiralled towards the year 2000.

In 1997 and 1998, I attended UFO conventions and talks, chatting with and interviewing various UFO fans, discovering that UFOs were held in almost mystic reverence. I witnessed a lot of nodding and chin-stroking about the importance of particular sightings, coupled with a defensive paranoia ('What are "they" hiding from us?'), along with an 'Isn't Ireland great, we can now afford our own spacemen!' sense of celebration.

Around the country, something was definitely going on. UFOs were being seen all over the place: a spate of them from the Wicklow Mountains, recurring sightings near Bantry, and a giant black triangle that flew over Sligo. That last one appears to have been have been a hoax by a 'Hans Rosenthal', and unconnected to the craft that crashed at some point in the nearby Curlew Mountains, where the security forces were involved in a major cover-up. Who was the mysterious disgruntled Garda who spilled the beans? The list of UFO reports from this time is too long to recount here.

I first wrote an article on UFOs for Blather.net in May 1997, following reports from Coomhola, near Bantry, West Cork. A British television team had apparently filmed UFOs there, while making a TV series called *We are Not Alone*. Cigar-, cylinder- and diamond-shaped objects, and on some occasions, 'balls of light' were reported. On hand were people from the Irish Centre for UFO Studies (ICUFOS - great acronym!) and PEIR (Programme for Extraterrestrial Intelligence Research). In the coming months, I kept track of these two apparently allied groups. While ICUFOS's Alan Sewell had a more 'nuts-and-bolts' approach to UFOs and was pretty much a UFO fan, it emerged that PEIR had a rather more esoteric approach, claiming that the sightings were of 'light beings' or *merkabah*, a Hebrew word meaning 'chariot' that first appears in Ezekiel 1:4-26, referring to the throne-chariot of God. The spokesman for PEIR, astronomer and telescope-builder Eamon Ansbro, however, described his idea of *merkabah* as 'energy constructs', saucer-shaped energy fields some fifty-five feet in diameter. Ansbro, speaking later at a UFO conference in Wynn's Hotel, Dublin, demonstrated this as being a Star of David shape, with a person inside (not unlike Da Vinci's *Vitruvian Man*).

As time went on, I published more UFO reports on Blather.net, all somewhat sceptical, some scathing, and I received phone calls from people who'd seen things in the sky. Not having a car at the time meant I couldn't really travel to investigate, but when attending a UFO conference in Cork City, I ended up sitting up talking weirdness till the wee hours in a hostel room with Sewell and Ansbro. They, and their friends, were full of stories about alien abductions, missing time phenomena and UFO sightings. The stories were bizarre, but extremely intriguing.

In further encounters with Ansbro, I found that he claimed to predict flurries of UFO sightings, using a concept called 'Astronautical Theory', created by a Roy Dutton. This involved a few major leaps of faith, like the idea that a huge mothership was hanging out somewhere outside our atmosphere, shooting 'probes' into the atmosphere along arbitrary 'flight paths'. In the case of Ireland, these paths intersected in three places: Bantry in West Cork, Boyle in County Roscommon, and right above Dublin. Apparently these intersections were the optimum places to see UFOs, presumably because they were like intergalactic roundabouts for aliens. It sounded suspiciously like an aerial rip-off of the New Age 'energy' gobbledegook spouted about 'ley lines'. Ley lines have a more mundane, yet still interesting origin: Alfred Watkins coined the term in 1921, to describe the apparent alignments between ancient sites in Britain. He said nothing at all about 'energy'. Don't get me started…

But back to the flight paths. I spent Sunday evening, 14 December 1997, on Bull Island, in the suburbs of Dublin. With me in the sand dunes were some members of ICUFOS and PEIR, watching the sky with binoculars and cameras. Ansbro wasn't there; he was at Boyle, with some of the local UFO fans. Tonight was the night: Eamon had announced that there would be UFOs seen over Dublin, Roscommon and Cork.

The watchers watched the skies. I watched the watchers. Every time a light appeared on the eastern horizon, the group trembled with excitement. The light would grow, rising in the sky, then break up into several lights, one green, one red, with a big white one in the middle. Then the sound would start - *woosh* - and another passenger jet would come in for landing at Dublin airport. The UFO-watchers would slump with disappointment, but bounce back as soon as a new light appeared. We had the flight paths alright, but unfortunately, the craft were of terrestrial origin.

Journalists came and went in the course of the night, including, strangely enough, a reporter from *Woman's Way*. Naturalist and artist Don Conroy swung by for a chat. René, one of the UFO watchers, did a phone interview with Chris Barry on his late night talk show.

As the night wore on, lights *did* appear: meteors streaked across the heavens, as part of the annual Geminid meteor shower. I felt it must be more than a coincidence that an astronomer like Ansbro would choose 14 December as a prime night for seeing UFOs, when surely he was aware that there was a meteor shower around this date every year. I smelled a rat.

Later, I got the DART back to the city centre with some of the UFO fans. They were mostly despondent; there had been no UFOs. I listened in to Chris Barry on my radio while on the train. People started frantically phoning in about a strange star-like light hanging directly over Dublin Bay, which seemed to be flickering different colours. Barry looked out his studio window, and said that he could see it, but it looked like a normal star. Alan Sewell was still on the line, and he reported that he could see it too in Roscommon and that it was only the star, Sirius. This wasn't good enough for some people though, who phoned in maintaining that their UFO was 100 times bigger than any star!

A week later, I bumped into one of the disappointed UFO watchers who told me that 'amazing things' had appeared on the photographic film they had shot that night on Bull Island. I never did see those photographs, which probably prevented an embarrassing situation.

Personally, I don't really mind what people believe in: God, giant white rabbits, Pat Kenny or crop circles. But I didn't like the idea that someone could be blatantly misleading the public, or at least the UFO-believing section of the public. So I wrote about the meteor showers in Blather.net.

I'd already received some letters of complaint from another fantastically-named organization: IUFOPRA, the Irish UFO and Paranormal Research Assocation, after delivering a critical review of their UFO conference in Dublin. Since I had started challenging Ansbro's predictions, my relationship with ICUFOS and PEIR faded away too. I was the unbeliever, and could no longer be accommodated.

Nevertheless, I was later scheduled to speak at a science-fiction conference in Dun Laoghaire, on a UFO panel with Sewell. On the morning of the event he pulled out, apparently claiming that I would just twist his words. I found this amusing, as I probably *would* have twisted his words somewhat, but also because it suggested that he didn't feel his claims were watertight. About a year after the night on Bull Island, coming up to 14 December, Ansbro in a phone conversation invited me to Roscommon for a skywatch. I couldn't make it due to other commitments, but enquired about a Dublin watch. He said there wasn't one, but the next day I was on Today FM with Roscommon UFO-watcher Betty Myler. It transpired in the course of the interview that there *had* been a Dublin watch the night before, on Bull Island again. I had been officially uninvited.

Eventually, I became bored with UFOs. I'd read everything from Carl Jung's *Flying Saucers*, which covers the symbolic and psychological aspects of the phenomenon, to some dreadful books sent to me for review. I'd had enough. I didn't feel I was learning anything new; in a short space of time I had gone in one side and out the other. I drifted out of the UFO scene. I'm sure the anal probes and cattle mutilations are doing just fine without me.

Dave Walsh

Postscript: Blather.net still occasionally covers UFO stories, especially if there is some interesting motif that escapes the usual run of UFO sightings. There's still a strong Irish fanbase out there, despite the lack of mainstream coverage, with websites like www.irishufology. net and Betty Myler's www.ufosocietyireland.com.

In 2006, *Conspiracy of Silence: UFOs in Ireland* by Dermot Butler and Carl Nally was published, which pushes the theory that the Irish government is covering up the truth about UFOs. I gave it a fairly scathing review both in *Fortean Times* and on Blather.net, which elicited a review of my review from some character called Val Young. Remarkably, his review of my review was actually longer!

Full disclosure: Blather.net and Dave Walsh are both part of the conspiracy, in the pay of the Irish government and other organizations, in a campaign to cover up the truth about UFOs. Believe nothing you read on Blather.net.

Visit http://blather.net/ufo for the full stories mentioned in this chapter.

SLOW WALKING
BANNED IN DUBLIN

Breaking news on Blather.net, 11 June 2003:

No more semi-loitering for tourists: a group of traders in the Grafton Street/Nassau Street area of Dublin have called for a minimum walking speed to be introduced. The group estimates that more than €100 million is being lost annually due to 'slow walking'.

'It gets especially bad in June,' said a spokesman, owner of a business on Nassau Street.

> People can't go out to buy lunch, or to meetings. Once the tourists arrive, no-one can get up or down the street, it all grinds to a halt. These people may walk like this in their own country, but they should be informed that the people of Dublin are not on their holidays.

The group has also called on Dublin City Council to introduce a network of 'speed cameras' for pedestrians at busy junctions like the bottom of Dawson Street. They suggest that mandatory fines would be imposed in order to decrease the amount of 'semi-loitering' which is allegedly taking place.

* * *

I wrote this story after a warm lunchtime in Dublin's main shopping area, unaware of a similar 'lane system' suggested for London's Oxford Street. After trying to fight my way up Nassau Street between the shuffling green slacks of geriatric American tourists, I retreated to my desk, where I banged out a few frustrated paragraphs of quick and dirty satire. Hours later, my mobile phone rang: it was a journalist asking me was the story true. I was so surprised that I answered 'No' – but he went ahead and published it anyway, in the *Daily Mirror*, if I correctly recall. A day later, a colleague and I, working in the production department of the short-lived *Dublin Daily* newspaper, 'caught' the story coming through, after one of our own journalists had picked up on it. We gently softened the story with an 'apparently', lest we get in trouble.

Even now, more than four years later, I meet people who believe that Dublin traders really did call for a ban on slow walking. As I say, I didn't write this as a hoax: it started as satire, but somehow became truth.

The great irony is that at the same time, Blather.net was involved in some deliberate media hoaxes, via the online discussion forum P45.net, run by friends of ours. It started out innocently enough, when someone posed the question 'How easy it would it be to start an urban legend?' The idea gathered momentum, and as Paul Clerkin and Mick Cunningham, the owners of P45.net, reported, by summer 2003:

> We were able to plant three stories in three different national publications…. Initially, we were thinking along the lines of a predictable kind of [Urban Legend]; the type that always involves anonymous people in anonymous places, a myth that is structured like a joke or an anecdote. But what people started coming up with instead were a lot more specific: fake media stories, written like genuine news stories in conventional 'journalese'…most P45ers had the general impression that they would take weeks or even months to go around the block and come back again. In fact it was a matter of hours or even minutes. People on the [discussion] boards were also surprised at how the mainstream media picked up on the hoaxes and ran them with very few changes. What was most disturbing was not just how willing the mainstream media were to run with complete hoaxes, but how some embellished and even claimed ownership of the stories.

The first hoax was simple, but clever. A news report told of an Irish brother and sister holidaying in the US, who were arrested in Springfield, Illinois, after 'anti-terrorist' police overheard them speaking a 'strange language'. The language, of course, was Gaelic. It's a story that's too good to be true: a bit of paddyism mixed with post 9/11 paranoia. It got picked up by the tabloids in Ireland. Then, according to Paul and Mick, 'the Daily Mirror decided to develop the story and added quotes from the mythical pair as if they had interviewed them. Even more incredible were the reports of people from Cobh admitting to knowing the arrested duo'.

After the papers in Springfield started running the story, there was no stopping the P45ers. Remember any of these? 'The Monaghan Association in New York in St Patrick's Day Parade Row', because their Monaghan banner looked like a map of Iraq. 'Mysterious Underground Tunnels found under Clontarf', by workers on the port tunnel: this was quoted in a recent local history book. 'Liam Lawlor - the Movie', starring Anthony Hopkins and Colin Farrell as young Liam. The *Irish Independent* ran the best one of all on the front page: 'Berlusconi Demands Immediate Repatriation of "Ireland's" Caravaggio'''. Silvio Berlusconi's office in Rome had to issue denials on that one.

That's the one that got the hoaxers caught. A researcher for RTE Radio 1's *5-7 Live* just had to Google the words Berlusconi, Caravaggio and Ireland and follow the evolution of the stories on a public discussion board. Any other journalist could have found this, if they'd bothered. Paul Clerkin ended up on *5-7 Live*, and the *Irish Independent* had to publish a front-page retraction of the story.

Mick and Paul wrote that:

> While planting our stories, we discovered just how much the various print and broadcast media feed off each other. Such is the constant push for new material on radio stations, many programmes don't bother to check emails that are sent in to the presenter. These emails are then read out as fact. The original Springfield legend made the radio and breaking news sites within an hour or two.

LEPREPORN

So here I am, sitting staring at an email in my inbox. It would seem that I'm being offered a part in a porn movie, which will pay €2,000 for one and a half hours' 'work'. Looking closer at the email, I see the company is called Lepreporn.

How did this all come about?

Some weeks previously I received a call from my agent, telling me I'd been successful in an audition for a part in a TV film. This was on one condition, that I had a full driving license. The part was too good to pass up, so I told them I would have it in time for filming. I hadn't been driving for years, and as I originally learned in a rusty twenty-five-year-old truck, this was going to take some work. I only had two months to undertake this challenge. I realized that this was going to be a costly exercise as lessons would be expensive. I needed some money, and I needed it fast. I started looking for extra work, but didn't have much luck.

Wondering what to do next, it occurred to me to try a money-drawing spell. I hadn't been doing any magick for a long time, so I knocked out a simple spell, almost carelessly. I asked for a specific amount, thinking I could sort out another few things I needed at the same time.

On a visit to Dublin two days later, I called around to see a friend. While checking my email on their computer, I saw there was a mail from net-model.com. This is a website for models and actresses, where you can display some photos and information, and then can be contacted by interested photographers. The site seems reputable, but I'm not sure that everyone who uses it is. The email was from a company called 'Lepreporn' offering me the exact amount I had asked for in my spell. They were offering me €2,000 for a three-day shoot, 'working' for a half an hour a day. I looked at their profile on the model site, and their blurb said:

> We are the only Irish adult film company which film R18 movies, we only employ Irish actors. We have been making movies for about 2 years now and are becoming major players in the adult industry so if you want to make good money and have lots of fun, email us your details.

'We only use Irish actors'. Is that supposed to be encouraging? They may have been stating that they are supporting only Irish workers, but really, the last thing you would want when making a porn movie is to 'bump' into someone you know. 'Oh, how ye Pat, are you working on this thing too? Oh great, it's nice to know someone else. I'll see you during the shoot then.'

Not to mention the chances of good old Irish porn being watched by someone who knows you. When I did a search on Google for Lepreporn, I came up with nothing. All I found was a page on windycitymedia.com which has David J. Madziarz pondering on the lack of leprechaun porn on the web. He says: 'The wee little ones must have given up sex for Lent because in spite of numerous Google searches, I couldn't find any leprechaun porn sites on the Internet. If it did exist, would it be called "lepreporn"?'

Mr Madziarz is quite right to feel disappointed at the lack of leprechaun porn, but I doubt Lepreporn are going to fill the gap in the market. Unless of course this is Mr Madziarz's company... in which case there will be some interesting costumes for the 'actors' to wear in the films.

I am afraid I will have to disappoint (or not) a few readers by saying I declined the offer. If I ever feel the urge to make a porn film, it will be as far away as possible (Mars perhaps). I felt the universe or whatever was having a right old laugh at me messing with spells.

Next time I'm getting it right. No half measures.

Oh and I did get my money in the end. Just not that way.

Suzanne Walsh

ANGRY DREAMS

Occasionally I have dreams during which I get extremely angry with people for whom I feel no anger in 'real life', and wake up somewhat disturbed and embarrassed. It happened again last night (I was in a theatre in Venice pelting the collective Blather.net readership with Monster Munch, while shouting and laughing hysterically.) [What were you doing there anyway, you contemptible scum?]. I decided to use the web to investigate the phenomenon of angry dreams.

A search for 'angry dreams' first turned up a commercial website called Absolute Comfort,[1] selling beds and mattresses etc. Their anger page (yes, they have an anger page) revealed something that seemed to me very sensible indeed: '…what about angry dreams? It's obvious that we go to bed tired at night. We wake up refreshed, rested and energized the next morning. The body using its built-in intelligence knows how to relieve itself of fatigue and accumulated stress and strain from the day's activities.' Yes, I was completely exhausted when I hit the hay last night, and these angry dreams must have been the release of stress and strain.

The web search also brought me to a blog called Comfortable Disorientation[2] that seemed to confirm this. A woman on holidays was having angry dreams in which she was:

> raging in a way I have never done in real life (or at least not since I was a toddler)…Each morning I woke up feeling replenished and renewed, yet amused and rather embarrassed about my hysterics…

I'm assuming it was some kind of reaction against the last few weeks, which have been unusually hectic.

It wasn't clear to me whether the anger of these dreamers was directed against people or situations they genuinely felt angry about in 'real life'. I would say that it doesn't matter in the dream who the anger is directed against, it is just the body releasing strain. But an article on sleepandhealth.com,[3] stating generally that '...angry dreams can produce appropriate emotional channels for releasing bad feelings and relieving stress' went on to specify that: 'Research by Dr. Rosalind Cartwright demonstrated that if divorced women had angry dreams about their ex-husbands, these women recover faster from post-divorce depression.' So maybe sometimes the anger is 'real'.

Jungians on gesher.org[4] are even more convinced about the reality of the anger. They say, 'you might see yourself acting angry in a dream. As you consider this, you understand that this is part of yourself that you already know about, your poor control over your temper.' This literal interpretation seems inevitable in Jungian theory; because anytime you *yourself* appear in a dream it's the 'part of yourself that you already know about'. This is part of Jungian shadow theory: 'the idea that each of us have parts of our ego that we have rejected because of our upbringing environment, family, and parental influence' and that we encounter these shadow parts in our dreams as unfamiliar people. But believing this would seem to commit me to ascribing a great deal of reality to everything *I* do in a dream.

The website called Dream Moods[5] doesn't impress me much either. Again, they are very literal: 'Being angry in your dream may have been carried over from your waking life. In your dream, you may have a safe outlet to express such emotions. You may have some suppressed anger and aggression that you have not consciously acknowledged.' Hmm, am I not bad-tempered enough, that I have suppressed anger too?

In the same paragraph there is another striking assumption – of prophetic abilities: 'To dream that you are feeling much anger, forewarns that you will be involved in a terrible and tense situation. Your loved ones will let your down and disappoint you. It also forewarns that once solid ties will be broken.' Er, yeah, thanks, what a positive thing to say.

Strangely, I find myself most reassured by the capitalists who set up their website to sell pillows. I know that Blather.net readers might be inclined more to reading Jungians and 'specialist' dream sites but don't bother unless you want to feel shit about yourselves.

Love to you all.

Barry Kavanagh

(1) Absolute Comfort's anger page
http://www.absolutecomfortonsale.com/a-go-to-bed-angry.html
(2) Comfortable Disorientation blog
http://comfortabledisorientation.typepad.com/my_weblog/2006/07/angry_
dreams.html
(3) Article on sleepandhealth.com
http://www.sleepandhealth.com/Newspaper/2004/April/10.htm
(4) Dream interpretation on gesher.org
http://www.gesher.org/Dreams,%20Visions,%20and%20Prophecy/
Dream%20Interpretation.htm
(5) Dream Moods
http://www.dreammoods.com/dreamthemes/feelings.htm

THERE ARE NO KANGAROOS
IN AUSTRIA

Ireland has no native marsupials, yet somehow, animals resembling kangaroos get reported here. The 'explanations' vary: rabbits, hares, deer, chupacabras, lake monsters and even aliens. On 2 December 2003, Blather.net received an email from someone calling themselves 'Vercingetorix', who had been out in the Dublin/Wicklow Mountains, near the junction of Killakee and Cruagh roads, for a walk. At about 4.15, when it was getting dark, she caught a 'white flash' out of the corner of her eye. Thinking that it was too large to be a hare or rabbit, she noted that it was 'moving kangaroo style'.

> I've seen Kangaroos in Australia, and the movement was definitely very similar. However the white flash on the animal's rump seemed much bigger than that on the grey kangaroos I remember. The backside of the animal seemed too broad to be a deer. It didn't seem to be kangaroo-like in appearance, especially since it seemed to be using its fore limbs for support. However, when it moved it definitely jumped kangaroo style. I then realized there were two and moved slowly towards them. However, they seemed very timid and skipped away even though I was a good bit away. The last I saw was the white rump flash disappear into dense conifers. Is there a kangaroo farm in the Dublin/Wicklow mountains? Could it be a fallow deer?… Or some kind of strange cryptozoological mystical monster?

While there are no kangaroo 'farms' that I've heard of in Ireland in terms of meat production, there have been several locations where kangaroos have been kept in zoos around the country. I doubt that the damp, cold climate, and heather and conifer vegetation of the Dublin/ Wicklow Mountains would afford much in the way of food or comfort for 'roos. However, fallow and sika deer (introduced by the Normans in 1244, and by Lord Powers to Powerscourt, Wicklow in 1860) live wild in these mountains and both sport a white rump patch, which is quite distinctive during the winter, when both species are in their winter colours. Having seen both kinds of deer in the mountains over the years, I can say that both species 'bounce' over heather in what could be mistaken for a 'kangaroo-like' manner. Case closed, we hope.

That's not to say that marauding mobs of kangaroos aren't roaming the Irish countryside. The *Irish Independent* of 12 January 2007 reported that:

> Gardaí were called in yesterday to try to trace a missing kangaroo in the West. The brown two-year-old kangaroo escaped from a field in Co. Roscommon on Sunday evening and has not been seen since; to its owner's distress. The animal was being cared for as a pet in a field at Crennane, between Ballaghaderreen and Loughglynn. However, he escaped on Sunday evening and there have been no reports of any sightings since then.

This creature may still be at large; we never heard any more about it at the Blather.net newsroom.

On 20 July 2006, Reuters reported that a kangaroo named Sydney had gone AWOL from a circus in Kinsale, County Cork. Somehow, along the way, Sydney was renamed Hoppy, by the locals. Farmer John Walsh (no relation to this writer) was pretty philosophical: 'He would be happy out there and he'll have plenty of grass, plenty of water and plenty of sunshine,' Walsh told Reuters, as Ireland basked in hot weather more typical of Sydney's native Australia. In his investigative report, Blather.net's Damien was not unconcerned:

> Rumours abound about what will become of Hoppy. Fine Gael rushed out an urgent statement this morning, quickly scotching

rumours that Hoppy would be running for local office. Ronan Keating was heard on local radio, claiming that he and Hoppy had been in a teenage boy-band together – and explaining that the Aussie had to go after a difficult incident involving a key, the side of some-one's car, a psychotically jealous female 'roo and a handycam-filmed romp with an unnamed Irish wallaby. Former heavyweight boxing champion Steve Collins was said to be lining up a fifteen-round bout in the Phoenix Park and Chelsea Football Club have dispatched six Russian heavies, armed with hammers, bananas and a suitcase stuffed with sixteen million pounds.

Do kangaroos eat bananas? Do they hold kangaroo courts? We heard no more about this 'roo either; it may now be in cahoots with the Beast of Ballaghaderreen. Or the Achill Island monster, which made the front page of the *Evening Herald* on 4 June 1968, thanks to some dubious polaroid photography by an unnamed and untraceable travelling business man, apparently from County Louth. I've only seen a poor microfiche copy, but that photograph seemed to show a fake lizard stuck in a tree. Before this kerfuffle, however, there were local sightings: Gay Dever, a fifteen-year-old witness, said that 'it was much bigger than a horse, black in colour with a long, slender and sheep-looking head, long neck and tail. It moved like a kangaroo and its hind legs were bigger than the front ones'. I've researched the Achill monster quite a bit, and I still have no idea what was going on there.

Whatever about the Irish, it's the Austrians I feel sorry for, always getting confused with Germans and Australians. And like the Australians, the Alpine Aussies have got 'roos now too. On Wednesday, 14 May 2003, *Yahoo News* reported the death of a kangaroo in a hit-and-run incident in Steyr, after it had apparently escaped from its owner. On 16 March 2006, another kangaroo (unnamed) escaped in Austria, before being discovered on a country road about three miles outside the town of St Veit in the province of Carinthia, where it evaded police capture, until sedated by a local vet. Apparently one can now buy t-shirts that read 'There are no kangaroos in

Austria'. They're lying, of course: there's an Australian Football Club in Austria called the Vienna Kangaroos.

In Germany, a kangaroo called Skippi escaped from a private zoo in Baden-Württemberg, Bavaria (not Austria or Australia) in August 2007, making it to the Allgäu until it got run over by a truck close to Memmingen.

A 1997 issue of *Fortean Times* (FT 103) had an article entitled 'There's a Flyin' Marsupial', which reported on the plethora of kangaroo sightings in Sweden. But Swedish zoos were apparently missing no 'roos, and Swedish law doesn't permit the ownership of foreign wild animals that may survive in the wild.

More recently, on 30 October 2007, Danish police were appealing for help to track down a kangaroo that escaped from its owner's home in Copenhagen. Two had escaped, but one had decided to come home by itself. The last we heard (according to AP) was that the missing animal had been spotted, and its owner was on the way to the rescue. 'He is very nice,' said the owner, Jan Passer, 'and easy to cajole with just a carrot.'

In the United States, cryptozoologist Loren Coleman has kept tabs on kangaroo activity. In his 1983 book *Mysterious America*, the reports include the kangaroo with a hard kick, leaving two policemen with bruised shins in Chicago's Northwest Side in 1974, while no kangaroos were reported missing; and 'a giant kangaroo' sighted in South Pittsburg, Tennessee in 1934, allegedly killing and partially devouring a few German Shepherds. This is a dubious one: kangaroos are herbivores.

Finally, when I tell people that Lambay, a small Island off the coast of Dublin, has a feral colony of wallabies (smaller relations of the kangaroo), as does the Isle of Man, I tend to get a stony, sceptical stare. Fair enough, really. You don't need to believe everything we tell you, even if it's true.

Dave Walsh

THE TOMB OF GOD

Review of the book by Richard Andrews and Paul Schellenberger.

Ah, the Rennes-le-Château mystery! Often discussed around the fireplace at the Blather Wolves' Lodge in Connecticut, glasses of (expensive) port in hand. *Did* the priest Bérenger Saunière (1852–1917) find something hidden in Rennes-le-Château, his parish in the South of France, in the late nineteenth century? Not long after he arrived in the area in 1885, he suddenly became rich, and funded renovations of the Church of Mary Magdalene, inscribing the cryptic statement *Terribilis est locus iste* above the front door.

The mystery, although solved in 1910 (see below), has seeded a huge industry in conspiracy theories. Blather.net editors' interest was piqued somewhat in the wake of the bestseller *The Holy Blood and the Holy Grail* (1982) but was off-peak by the time *The Da Vinci Code* (2003) made wild speculations about the bloodline of Christ *de rigeur* in sports halls and beauty salons across the globe. As you no doubt know, *The Holy Blood and the Holy Grail* suggested that Saunière discovered parchments proving that the head of the secret society the Priory of Sion was the descendant of Jesus Christ, and we can't ignore suggestions like that at Blather HQ, neither in our Toronto office nor in our ramshackle hut in Montmartre. No, not at all.

At some point between the *Holy Blood* and *Da Vinci Code* eras, we took to reading some of the many books being churned out on this topic. We picked one at random, *The Tomb of God* by Richard

A Load of Blather

Andrews and Paul Schellenberger, and gave it a thorough going over. Here's the text of that review.

★   ★   ★

Certain parchments were published in 1967 by Gérard de Sède, purporting to be parchments that Saunière is rumoured to have found. These are supposed to have been hidden by Antoine Bigou, resident priest at Rennes-le-Château at the time of the French Revolution. Andrews and Schellenberger believe that a geometric analysis of the parchments reveals that they are maps. However, the correspondence of these to twentieth-century maps shows that the parchments could not be the ones Saunière is supposed to have discovered. Nevertheless, the authors contend that they *are* genuine, except that they have been 'tampered with' (by Saunière? Or de Sède?).

Another rumour about Saunière is that he went to the Louvre to get copies made of three paintings. These are (1) Nicolas' Poussin's second version of *Les Bergers d'Arcadie*, painted some time in the 1630s; (2) another seventeenth-century painting, *Saint Anthony and Saint Paul* by David Teniers the Younger; and (3) the sixteenth-century *Coronation of Pope Celestine V* by artist unknown. These share a certain geometry, which Andrews and Schellenberger applied to an old map of the area around Rennes-le-Château, revealing to them the 'site', which they identify as Mount Cardou, where they think that whatever made Saunière rich was or is buried. They claim to have examined many other paintings and only found two other significant examples of the geometry: *La Fontaine de Fortune* (an illustration from the fifteenth-century Grail romance *Le Cuer d'Amours Espris*) and a thirteenth-century circular map of Jerusalem from the Royal Library at The Hague. Does this show ongoing secret knowledge of the site from the thirteenth century onwards? Unfortunately, there's no more evidence offered.

Andrews and Schellenberger believe the 'site' contained or contains the remains of Jesus. On the one hand, they pour cold water on the work of Michael Baigent, Henry Lincoln and Richard Leigh (authors of *The Holy Blood and the Holy Grail*) and their insubstantial evidence for a bloodline flowing from Jesus through the Royal families of Europe to Pierre Plantard, the Grand Master of the Priory of Sion (devoting more specific negative criticism to Lincoln's *The Holy Place*, another book about the role of geometry in the Rennes-le-Château mystery); however, on the other hand they use *The Holy Blood and the Holy Grail* as a source for much of their historical information! Oh, no…

They believe that the Priory of Sion, de Sède's source for the parchments, consists of the cognoscenti of the Secret. They swallow the Priory of Sion's claim to be the same organization that existed in 1152, and the claim that the Splitting of the Elm at Gisors in 1188 had to do with them. The authors do attempt to answer the question of why the hell initiates into the Secret would spend their time putting out titbits of information for the likes of de Sède and Lincoln to misinterpret. They argue that by having speculation about the Priory of Sion's Secret in the public domain, its power is strengthened in French esoteric circles. That indeed may be true. No doubt all this stuff helps Plantard's career. However, knowing the fact that the Priory of Sion (est. 1956) is the source of not just the parchments but many of the stories about Saunière, is there any justification for believing any of it at all?

Then there's the conspiracy. Andrews and Schellenberger do not understand that hermetic symbolism is shared by different groups throughout history for intellectual, aesthetic and spiritual reasons, not because there are direct links between historically separated groups or that there is some physical Secret (such as the location of the body of Jesus) of which every Tom, Dick and Templar from the Gnostic Gospels to the Rosicrucian Manifestos is an initiate.

To what purpose was this body of Jesus put? A & S think it was useful as a defence of Gnostic doctrine against Pauline doctrine. Well, considering the fate of the former and the success of the latter, obviously it wasn't much of a defence. After Gnosticism disappeared, it survived in different forms through the hermetic tradition, though not, as A & S think, continuously.

It is also worth remembering that not every group condemned by the Church was heretical. Chapter eighteen of this book assumes that the heresies ascribed to the Knights Templar during their persecution have their basis in fact. Senior Templars confessed to all sorts of absurdities under torture but then so did the Guildford Four and Birmingham Six. *Baphomet* is nonsensical both as a word and as a supposed Templar deity. I would refer anyone interested in the suppression of the Knights Templar to chapter five of Norman Cohn's *Europe's Inner Demons - the Demonization of Christians in Medieval Christendom* for the facts.

Furthermore, I cannot overlook the description in chapter seventeen of Qumran (where the Dead Sea Scrolls were found) as a settlement of Essenes. It was not. The Essenes were pacifists, whereas archaeological data indicates that Qumran was a military site, defending the road into Jerusalem. The Essenes were ascetics, so why are there are graves of women and children, i.e. families, at Qumran? Also, the fact that these graves are oriented north-south, in the Roman style, means they were not buried by their own people. It was not a cemetery; it was the aftermath of a massacre of Jews by Roman soldiers when they took Qumran. Interestingly, if there hadn't been such pseudo-Christian enthusiasm for erroneously believing Qumran to be a religious settlement, Bishop James Pike would not have accidentally died in the desert on his quest-like journey there in 1969, the subject of Philip K. Dick's last novel, *The Transmigration of Timothy Archer*, an enjoyable topic of discussion on many of our desert camel-rides through Blather's Research Area 52.

I should add that the Dead Sea Scrolls themselves are by no means the 'testimony to the true origins of Christianity' that A & S say they are. Even a cursory look at academic studies of the scrolls will make this obvious.

The most entertaining part of *The Tomb of God* is concerned with the fate of the remains of Jesus. With one story – about a preserved mummy hidden in the Languedoc region – Andrews and Schellenberger can only provide myth and legend as a source. With another story – that Jesus and his family lived in the region on estates owned by Herod – the 'convincing' (i.e. highly dubious) writings of Barbara Thiering are given as a source.

I think you get the idea. More holes than a pack of polo mints.

★ ★ ★

And oh yes, the solution of the mystery: Saunière was allowed take donations of a franc or two for saying requested masses and prayers for the dead. He was supposed to say a maximum of three masses a day, but he advertised, and managed to sell hundreds more masses than he could possibly ever say. *Terribilis est locus iste* means 'this place is awesome'. No doubt Saunière thought it was pretty awesome, seeing as he was raking it in. The fraud resulted in the ecumenical trial of both Saunière and his bishop in 1910-11, and their careers ended in disgrace.

Barry Kavanagh

LUCY DELL

In 2003, guest Blather.net writer Oliver Bayliss (current whereabouts unknown) went down to the dell to find something rotten:

The south of Warwickshire is considered to be one of the most scenic areas of England, maintaining its picturesque appeal without succumbing to parody. While the north of the county is dominated by the Isengard landscapes of Birmingham and Coventry, the south remains peaceful, cultured and preserved, with Shakespeare's birthplace of Stratford-Upon-Avon lovingly at its heart. Historic castle towns such as Kenilworth and Warwick offer civilization at its most decorous between the blonde wheat fields and nicely understated hedgerows. Even the roughest streets of Leamington Spa would appear to a passing Londoner so clean and lacking in human rubble as to suggest that a royal visit must be due the following day. Of course, dotted about are the rampant pustules of Little Chefs, KFCs, Slug and Lettuce pubs and Blockbuster Videos that one must expect these days but even they fail to rupture the static serenity. However, there is something rotten in Shakespeare's county.

On Thursday, 20 August this year, *The Courier*, the local newspaper of Leamington Spa, ran a short article on the disappearance of a fifteen-year-old girl named Sophie Wager. Details were sketchy; Sophie's parents had last seen their only daughter on the seventeenth of that month, when she had left home at around noon with a couple of girlfriends on a bicycle ride through the Warwickshire countryside. The girls were riding close to the banks of the river

Avon an hour later when Sophie exclaimed that she had forgotten about something and turned back, racing off before her friends could even say goodbye. That night, one of the girls, after being unable to connect to Sophie's mobile, rang the Wager household to talk to her and swiftly induced panic; Sophie had not returned home and nobody knew where she was. After two days of frantic searching by her parents across the countryside, no trace of Sophie was found. The article concluded with a plea written by Mrs Wager, asking anyone who had seen her daughter to contact her.

In the subsequent issue of *The Courier*, dated 27 August, an editorial footnote declared Sophie Wager had returned home on her bicycle on the night of the twenty-fourth, having been missing for a week. She was in good health, with no signs of under-nourishment or dehydration, and appeared utterly unharmed. Her clothes and hair were perfectly clean and both had evidently been washed during her disappearance. When asked where she had been, Sophie would only offer the rather cryptic reply, 'Down in the dell where we all fell'. Local police were said to be conducting an investigation.

The incident concerning Sophie Wager is but the latest in a discon-certingly unspoken series of vanishings among South Warwickshire teenagers, dating back decades and possibly even centuries. Cases of missing persons are of course very common but since being founded in 1832, *The Courier* has, on average, reported such a weeklong disappearance once every year, always during summer. In almost every case, when the reappeared and unblemished child was asked where he or she had been, the answer was some variant of 'down in the dell'. On 10 July 1973, as a typical example, fourteen-year-old Kulwant Dhinsay walked off from a family picnic outside Stratford and showed up seven days later on the family doorstep as if he had just popped out to the newsagent, explaining that he 'had to go to the dell'.

One can easily deduce that these vanishings have been little more than copycat cries for attention from spoilt brats, although extensive research into *The Courier* archives conjures up a curious pattern:

following each article concerning a disappearance to 'the dell', not only is there never any follow-up to the reappearance, reporting something like the findings of a police investigation, but the responsible journalist's name becomes conspicuously absent from the paper a few issues later. Attempts to contact Mr Ben Evans, the journalist who had covered the Sophie Wager story, were answered by *The Courier*'s receptionist with the unsettling information that Mr Evans had recently left the paper for a job with Sainsbury's Homebase. This is not at all inconceivable, considering the number of young transitory journalists who pass through local papers all over the country, and also that *The Courier* office is such a dispiriting Georgian cell that Homebase would probably feel like Rio in comparison.

Deeper research into county history at Warwick Public Library does however present a further curiosity: the only recorded place-name in the area associated with a 'dell' appears to be 'Lucy Dell', a small village that lies somewhere on the north-side bank of the Avon, among the old oaks and bluebells a little east of Stratford. However, ask any Warwickshire indigent if they have passed through, or even heard of Lucy Dell and chances are that they will just stare at you blankly. The history of the village, not to mention its precise whereabouts, appears to be shrouded in mystery. The name can be found in the Domesday Book, which states its vague riverside location in the Avon valley, reports a population of fourteen, and values it at a pricey 200 pence without an obvious explanation. An old Warwickshire rhyme entitled 'Midland Maids', from around AD 400 and still sung within some of the more rustic pubs of the county, also features the place, in the somewhat risqué line: 'I put me head down in Lucy's dell,/ Where fairies and all delights do dwell.'

It would seem that Lucy Dell has somehow maintained isolation from the present day. No roadmap or atlas seems to have the village marked. Inquires made to the West Midlands police, Royal Mail, BT, Stratford library, and the various gas, water and electricity companies covering the county all amounted to complete ignorance. Enquires made to Warwickshire County Council were met with bewildering incompetence, as did attempts to utilize the new directory

Del' constantly in endless personal letters thereafter, right up until his death in 1625, allegedly in a most vitriolic manner following the deaths of his son Prince Henry and wife Queen Anne. One of his final letters, written mere hours before his death, is said to be pages upon pages of the repeated phrase: 'I was luld down into her del, /Where I drank deple from her wel.'

Rumour, according to Levack, has it that James constantly pestered William Shakespeare about the area (who was also said to curse the place-name for somehow ruining one of his best plays) until his passing in 1616, going so far as to habitually burst into Shakespeare's London residence at night, royal guard in tow, raving about his vivid nightmares, and, even more unbelievably, once drunkenly confided to a chambermaid that Queen Elizabeth had forgiven Shakespeare for his part in the ill-fated Essex Rebellion because of a courtly fear of where he was from. Naturally, there is no documented evidence at all to support any of this.

So, is the fabled Lull Dell actually the elusive Lucy Dell? It's difficult to say, as they are equally inexplicable but one would suspect the village of Lucy Dell to have simply derived its name from lore, as have countless other English villages, and continue to radiate its mythical heat into the subconscious minds of those around it throughout history. This is somehow creating a problem: the contact number for the Wager family, as printed by *The Courier*, has been disconnected and no Wager family listed in the phonebook claim to have a Sophie; no local branch of Sainsbury's Homebase claim to employ any Ben Evans; the police evidently have no record of an entire village community; emails to the office of James Plaskitt, MP for Leamington and Warwick, go unanswered; the Avon woods remain untouched as protected land, yet neither the National Trust, English Heritage or the British Tourist Authority admit to any conservation in the area; and next summer, another random family may face seven days in Hell from the misuse of folklore by ungrateful offspring.

For your diligent correspondent, only one possibly productive course of action presents itself: a trek through the Avon woods, in search of Lucy Dell, packing plenty of silver bullets and weasel brains, to dispel its myth and naturalize its irrational fever once and for all.

The game's afoot.

Oliver Bayliss

F*CKING MAGIC

'Every man and woman is a star' – Aleister Crowley.

Sex magick? I got caught bandying about the phrase, like I knew what it meant, in front of Clare Taylor, the editor of *The Yoke* magazine. 'Great', she said. 'You can write an article for the magazine that explains it.' Disclaimer: I may not know what I'm talking about, but let's start with defining magic as a way of perceiving experiences in a way that goes beyond the mundane. And let's assume that we are all, or can be, magicians.

Long before the swinging 1960s or the rise of popular New Age culture, the English occultist Aleister Crowley published plenty of literature on ritual sex, disguising his thoughts in obtuse prose and verse. At the same time, artist and magician Austin Osman Spare also engaged the same subject, somewhat more lucidly than Crowley. Ahead of their time, they were vilified by early twentieth-century society for their attempts to elevate analysis and exploration of human sexuality from the scientific to a more spiritual realm. Both writers drew on the legacy of ritual sex, used in ancient civilizations to ensure the blessing of the gods for whatever purpose the participants in the ceremonies intended.

In pagan Ireland, childless women would apparently spend the eve of Lughnasa (1 August) on the summit of Croagh Patrick, encouraging fertility by spending a symbolic night with the god Lug. This demonstrates the main thrust of sex magick. The intensity of the real, simulated or symbolic sex or masturbation is used as a tool to focus on the object of desire. Spare's legacy includes the concept of sigil magic: 'magically charged' symbols, used to reach specific desires or intents, drawn or otherwise created by the magician. These sigils can be best absorbed via a state of euphoria attained through drugs, extreme fatigue, pain or sex.

Grant Morrison, best known for having written comics like *Doom Patrol*, *Arkham Asylum* and *The Invisibles*, wrote hilariously on the use of sigils. He argues that masturbating is a damned good way to focus the mind into an altered state of perception:

> The human body has various mechanisms for inducing brief 'no-mind' states. Fasting, spinning, intense exhaustion, fear, sex, the fight-or-flight response will all do the trick. I have charged sigils while bungee-jumping, lying dying in a hospital bed, experiencing a total solar eclipse and dancing to techno. All of these methods proved to be highly effective but for the eager beginner nothing beats the wank technique.

Another method of accessing sex magick involves engaging one's inner world. Rather than promoting change in the external world, sex is used as a form of meditation, a method of exploring the self, or to draw two or more people closer together. This type of exploration is the essence of Tantra. In our been-there-humped-that culture, a mention of Tantric sex usually provokes ribald commentary about Sting's love life, twelve-hour shagging sessions with no climaxes, buckets of lubricant, first degree burns and skin grafts. However, at its simplest and most realistic, Tantra is an offspring of Hinduism, a reactionary strand incorporating Buddhist teachings, recorded in Sanskrit. It's concerned with inclusiveness and seeing all parts of the body and mind as potentially good. Tantra deals with much more than sex, but as *this* story *is* about sex, it's worth noting that Tantric practices aim to use sensuality and orgasmic ecstasy in order to expand consciousness.

Sounds like a right old pile of hippy shit, doesn't it? But before we start drowning in New Age gobbledegook or start attempting to pinpoint our chakras, let's get back to basics. I suspect, following the logic used above, that any consensual sexual encounter has magical potential. I'm not talking about spells and broomsticks, rather it's a matter of finding what works, whatever gets us beyond the mundane. On a practical level, there's little point in getting naked to chant Crowleyian or Sanksrit texts at your untutored lover, in the hope that you'll both reach some altered state of consciousness. Well, she or he might, but it'll probably mean they've fallen asleep.

In conventional sex, even in long-term relationships, we tend to be steered by our self-consciousness. 'Am I going to come too soon?' or 'What if he gets scared if I scream during my orgasm, and thinks I'm a nutter?' This kind of rational thought, regardless of how irrational its content, inhibits the flow of true sensuality. We just can't let go fully and so withhold commitment, or are unable to communicate our feelings or thoughts. This isn't to say that this is bad sex, not at all. It can involve explosive orgasms, still mean intimacy between lovers, and is the cornerstone of many a relationship. But when two lovers trust each other, and feel comfortable with one other, they can transcend their egos, forget who they are, and become one, existing in the moment. For example, it's no secret that the less we worry about our orgasms, the less of a need to worry about coming or not coming. It happens to some of us, some of the time. On a good day, it might not even be clear to either partner which one of them is having the orgasm. Now, tell me this isn't magic.

We can do better for ourselves than just shagging like dumb animals. Sex, for most of us, tends to be orgasm-oriented. Perhaps take a broader view and embrace sex magick? Use sex to cast spells. Truly abandon yourself to the adventures of the inner world. It doesn't really matter what methods are used. It's the attitude and perspective of the lovers – the magicians – that matter. Whatever it is that turns you on. Just remember to treat your whole being as a sexual organ. Blow your minds.

Dave Walsh

(First published as "Could it be Magic?" in *The Yoke* #5)

WYRD!

Over the years at Blather.net, we have described many of the items we have covered as 'weird news'. Certainly we mean 'weird' in both its strict sense of uncanny or supernatural, like schools closing because of ghosts, as occurred in India in 2005-6; and in its colloquial sense of strange or incomprehensible, like the news story from Cincinnati in 2006 about a corpse propped in front of a TV for two years without anyone noticing. But did you know that 'weird' originally meant something entirely different?

The original word was a noun, whereas we use the word as an adjective (e.g. 'Barry is weird') or an adverb (e.g. 'Barry is acting weird') *and* it was originally spelled wyrd.

To understand the concept of wyrd we need to look at history. Britain in the late Roman Empire was Christian, but from around AD 449 pagan Germanic tribes (Angles, Saxons and Jutes) invaded and settled. They brought pagan beliefs, as described in Old English literature and Tacitus' *Germania*. The Germanic tribes lived in a warrior-band based society. Life was seen as a hard struggle ending with a warrior's destiny (i.e. death). This fate was probably utterly meaningless, there being no conclusive evidence that the Anglo-Saxons believed in an after-life (like the warriors' Valhalla of Scandinavian mythology). The word for fate was wyrd, and that originally meant simply 'what happens'. So if somebody in those days had said 'That's wyrd!' they would have meant 'that's just the course of events'.

But reading Old English texts like *Beowulf* will not give you direct access to pagan beliefs. Christian missionaries spread Christianity through Britain, culminating in the Synod of Whitby in 664, and 'wyrd' came to acquire a Christian meaning. Even the pagan Danish invasions from 793 onwards did not halt the tide of Christianity; instead it ultimately resulted in English missionaries converting Scandinavia. Many pagan concepts continued in Christian form, and 'wyrd' came to mean destiny or fate as determined by almighty God.

Our 'weird', the adjective, first appeared in late Middle English, originally only preceding 'Sisters' in 'Weird Sisters'. The Weird Sisters are the Fates, the *Nornir* of Norse mythology. Their names are Urd, Verdandi and Skuld, the goddesses of the past, the present and the future, respectively. They dwell beneath the roots of Yggdrasil, the World Tree, and weave and spin everyone's fate, even the fates of the gods themselves. (As an interesting side-note, Old Norse and Old English have common roots as Germanic languages, and 'urd' is believed to come from the same root as 'wyrd').

The Weird Sisters appear in Shakespeare's *Macbeth* (first performed 1605 or 1606) and this accounts for the strong endurance of the word in Modern English. Examples in the *Oxford English Dictionary* of the meanings of weird between 1815 and 1820 include: 'of strange or unusual appearance, odd-looking'; 'partaking of or suggestive of the supernatural; of a mysterious or unearthly character'; and 'out of the ordinary course, strange, unusual; hence odd, fantastic'.

'Weird' as a noun survived beyond Old English. In 1470 it meant 'that which is destined or fated to happen; predetermined events collectively', but by 1814 it no longer meant fate, but 'a supernatural or marvellous occurrence'. It is now archaic, although I note that in Stephen Donaldson's *Chronicles of Thomas Covenant*, fantastic creatures called Waynhim have a concept of 'Weird', which means 'doom, destiny or duty'. We at Blather.net would be interested to know of any other uses of 'weird' in modern parlance that hark back to the old meanings of 'wyrd'.

Until then remember, when facing the zeitgeist or the shitegeist, 'weird' is just stuff that happens.

Barry Kavanagh

THE DALKEY BABY AND THE HOUSE OF HORRORS

For several weeks in the summer of 2005, the Irish media indulged itself in a feeding frenzy of tabloid hysteria, feasting on the gruesome story of 'Niamh' (now identified as 'Cynthia Owen'), who claimed that she had been the victim of abuse by an organized cabal of child-molesters during the 1970s. This resulted in her becoming pregnant whilst still a child herself, a crime allegedly facilitated by her parents. 'Niamh' then claimed to have watched as her new-born infant was stabbed to death with a knitting needle. In the wake of the 7/7 bombings in London, the story dropped off the media's radar: the last we heard being that an excavation (looking for the remains of an infant) in a Dublin garden, had revealed nothing. But, one year later, the story arrived back in the media, with the focus now shifted to the request for an excavation at a graveyard plot in Dublin. Blather.net followed the story carefully from the outset.

FALSE MEMORY SYNDROME

The full story details of the Dalkey Baby story are covered in detail on Blather.net in the original article from 2005. The key thing to note is that the claims at the heart of Cynthia Owen's story would appear to stem from 'memories' which were unearthed during 'regression therapy' in England. And as anyone who knows anything about the history of child-abuse hysteria will know, regression therapy is, to be quite blunt, a complete crock. More than that, it is a profoundly dangerous crock, which has led to the destruction of countless homes, families and lives.

The 'memories' which emerge from this therapy are, according to mainstream science, total bunkum, borne of what is now routinely referred to as 'False memory syndrome'. False memory syndrome is classified, by Dr. John F. Kihlstrom, professor of psychology at Yale University as follows:

> a condition in which a person's identity and interpersonal relationships are centered around a memory of traumatic experience which is objectively false but in which the person strongly believes. Note that the syndrome is not characterized by false memories as such. We all have memories that are inaccurate. Rather, the syndrome may be diagnosed when the memory is so deeply ingrained that it orients the individual's entire personality and lifestyle, in turn disrupting all sorts of other adaptive behavior. The analogy to personality disorder is intentional. False Memory Syndrome is especially destructive because the person assiduously avoids confrontation with any evidence that might challenge the memory. Thus it takes on a life of its own, encapsulated and resistant to correction. The person may become so focused on memory that he or she may be effectively distracted from coping with the real problems in his or her life.

THE PRETENCE OF SCIENCE

Whilst I have nothing but sympathy for Cynthia Owen (she has, quite clearly, suffered at length over this issue – whatever the truth of it), it's quite breath-taking that no-one from amongst the assembled coroners, journalists, policemen and lawyers who had an abundance of time to reflect on and research this issue, brought to light the issue of regression therapy and its centrality to this case. Regression therapy, according to all reputable sources consulted, is a dangerous branch of charlatanry, carried out by con-men, hucksters and New Age sensationalists masquerading under the pretence of science.

Lest you're concerned that these are my personal opinions, I'd draw your attention to a statement from the Royal College of

Psychiatrists which is freely available on Wikipedia:

> Psychiatrists are advised to avoid engaging in any 'memory recovery techniques' which are based upon the expectation of past sexual abuse of which the patient has no memory. Such...techniques may include drug-mediated interviews ['truth serum'], hypnosis, regression therapies, guided imagery, 'body memories', literal dream interpretation, and journaling. There is no evidence that the use of consciousness-altering techniques, such as drug-mediated interviews or hypnosis, can reveal or accurately elaborate factual information about any past experiences, including sexual abuse.

Those who have a vested interest in regression therapy might point to the fact that I have quoted extensively from the 'mainstream' mental health experts and have ignored or been intolerant of ideas from alternative medicine. To that end you might also have a look at the work of Doctor Ian Stevenson. Stevenson spent many years operating in areas of 'science' that undoubtedly raised the eyebrows of a few colleagues, concentrating as he largely did in trying to build a body of evidence to prove the veracity of reincarnation. But even he, a man with a very open mind, expressed concerns about regression therapy. He said:

> nearly all such hypnotically evoked 'previous personalities' are entirely imaginary just as are the contents of most dreams. They may include some accurate historical details, but these are usually derived from information the subject has acquired normally through reading, radio and television programs, or other sources. The subject may not remember where he obtained the information included, but sometimes this can be brought out in other sessions with hypnosis designed to search for the sources of the information used in making up the 'previous personality'. Experiments by E. Zolik and by R. Kampman and R. Hirvenoja have demonstrated this phenomenon.

JOURNALISM? WHAT JOURNALISM?

The case of the Dalkey Baby and the suffering of the Owen family is upsetting in the extreme. But this should not deter those in the business of reporting 'the news' (is such a term can even be used these days) to observe the simple fact that the entire episode has been borne of an utterly discredited, pseudo-scientific pile of nonsense. Once again, we must sadly observe, Irish journalists have manifestly failed in doing their jobs. And it's not like we're talking about a need for extensive research here: a simple Google search would have told the truth of this. But as we learned long ago (from the now notorious incident on P45.net where forum posters manufactured a fabricated news story about Silvio Berlusconi, which was printed by the Irish Independent), Irish journalism is in a shambolic state.

In an age when newspapers no longer seem to care for reporting the news, but rather concentrate on providing an audience to sell to advertisers, with deadlines driving an industry to parrot press-release after press-release, perhaps it's time to ask ourselves if most Irish broadsheets have any right to claim that they continue to employ 'journalists' at all.

Damien DeBarra

A GUIDE TO EASTER

When I was a small(er) girl, Easter was a time of great mystery. The statues in the church covered up, the gory story of Jesus' death, and the excitement of egg-hunting on Easter Sunday all added to the strange atmosphere of Easter week. It was perplexing, this mixture of crucifixions and chocolate. And what about having to kiss the statue of Jesus? That gave rise to a few strange nightmares I can tell you.

I have since become interested in the symbolism of that week, the death and rebirth themes which mirror nature's cycles, and how religion tries to express and explain them. These themes pre-date Christianity. In fact, the word Easter comes from the spring goddess Eostre, who gives her name to the female hormone oestrogen. The Easter bunny, originally a hare, is linked with the spring goddess and the moon, along with eggs, which symbolize fertility. Pagan or Christian, there are strange and sinister Easter traditions from the past centuries, which make ours seem mild by comparison.

Traditionally, Good Friday was meant to be a day of mourning, a day for fasting and prayer. However, because of the ban on working that day, it was far from gloomy for some individuals. Confusion also sprang from the name 'Good Friday'. This originally came from 'God's Friday'.

This has led to conflicting statements such as 'bread baked on Good Friday is lucky and cures all ills' but 'he who bakes or brews on Good Friday will have his house burnt down before the end of the year' (both from Northamptonshire 1851). Alternating views arise about being born on Good Friday, compounded by the belief in Ireland and England that Friday was the unluckiest day of the week. Therefore, 'the birth of a child on that day is very unlucky – indeed a birth on any Friday of the whole year is to be deprecated as a most unfortunate circumstance' (Wales 1880). While on a more positive note, 'unlucky to be born on a Friday, unless it is a Good Friday' (Lancashire 1870). Shedding blood on Good Friday is to be avoided:

> a story told me years ago by a former servant, which I recollect made a deep impression on me at the time. She told me how her father one Good Friday tried to kill a pig, notwithstanding the traditional unluckiness of the day; but in vain, as the pig would not die, and he was at length compelled to abandon the attempt for that day. (Devon 1883)

Washing on Good Friday was also frowned upon, explained by this Birmingham story from 1925: 'My mother always told me not to pour anything down the sink till after three o'clock on Good Friday, because the gutters of Jerusalem was running with our Lord's blood up till three o'clock.' Washing clothes was especially prohibited. Calamities could occur if this was not observed: clothes hung out to dry splattered with blood, or soapsuds turning red. There seemed to be a lot of Jesus' blood to go around. There was a danger that a member of the family could die from their clothes being washed on this day, because they were 'washed away'.

Easter Sunday traditions were perhaps more cheerful than Good Friday. The widespread belief in England and Ireland concerning 'sun dances' has all the connotations of a UFO sighting: 'To this pool the people used to come on Easter morning to see the sun dance and play in the water and the angels who were at the Resurrection playing backward and forwards before the sun' (Radnorshire). When the sun rises on Easter Sunday, it 'dances for joy'. This could be viewed either directly by gazing at the sky or through a pool or bucket of water. If the eager observer cannot see it, this is put down (conveniently) to a lack of faith, or the fact that the Devil always attempts to obscure the sight. But even animals celebrate this day, as this Irish belief from 1951 notes: 'Most of the beliefs in this country are traceable to Christian origins, the belief that donkeys kneel at the moment of sunrise on Easter morning, for instance, that they bray three times at sunrise on Good Friday.'

Other Irish Easter week customs include:

'Obtain new clothes for Easter Sunday' – in case any had been washed on Good Friday?

'Clean your house for Easter Sunday' – to remove any bloodstains, I presume.

'Maintain quiet on Good Friday from noon to 3pm' – useful while sleeping off a hangover from the night before.

'Cut your hair on Good Friday to prevent headaches in the year to come' – but if working is prohibited, where can a hairdresser be found?

And finally, make sure to 'die on Good Friday' as your rapid entry into Heaven is assured.

The most interesting, bizarre, and perhaps disturbing Easter custom in Ireland was 'The Procession of the Herring'. This was carried out in numerous Irish towns, symbolizing the end of Lenten abstinence. The procession was organized, and usually led by, the town butcher, who was probably glad to be back in business after Lent. In Dundalk, a herring was hung on a long stick and paraded through the town. This was followed by anyone who had suffered economically in the previous year. Carrying sticks, they would beat the herring into little pieces, before hurling what was left, along with insults, into the Castleton River. Decorating the stick with flowers and ribbons, the crowd would then make their cheery way home. In Drogheda it was called 'whipping the herring'. Here boys would tie dozens of herrings to a rope and drag them through the town, pursued by more boys armed with whips and sticks. In Cork, a single herring would be paraded through the city on a stick, while crowds shouted and jeered at the poor fish. Most people were delighted to see the end of fish dinners after Lent and glad to be eating meat once more.

Easter Monday was the day that Dublin people had their 'Funeral for a Fish', usually dressed in outlandish garments. What makes this violent and strange tradition even stranger is that nowadays the fish is a symbol for Jesus and Christianity. It was an odd reaction on a day that was meant to symbolize Jesus' rebirth.

This Easter, I will be tempting fate by trying out some of these superstitions: washing my clothes on Friday, cutting my hair and getting up early on Sunday to see the sun dance. And if you happen to see a girl running through the streets with a fish on a stick, it could be me.

Suzanne Walsh

CANNONBALLS FROM THE SKY

'There never was an explanation which didn't itself need to be explained' – Charles Fort.

In October 1997, a mystery cannonball crashed through the walls of a Missouri mobile home. Nobody knew where it came from, or who fired it. Amused, I wrote about it:

> A rather amusing, classically Fortean story crashed onto the Blather newsdesk this week, in the shape of a cannonball. The 'Civil War-type' missile tore through a window and two walls of Leonard and Kathy Mickelson's mobile home, in House Springs, Missouri, on Thursday night 16th of October, according to the Associated Press. Nobody was home when it happened, and the neighbours noticed nothing strange. Police are reportedly investigating the possible use of a small cannon, a weapon readily available for Civil War re-enactments. In an apparently unrelated incident reported by the Associated Press in Cincinnati, Ohio, on the 19th, a fourteen-year-old boy was severely injured by an exploding gunpowder charge during a Civil War re-enactment.

I continued the article by going off on a bizarre, whimsical tangent, sparked by Andy Silverman, a member of the Fortean mailing list[1] who suggested that the 'Civil War-type' projectile plummeted from Fort's hypothetical heavenly Super-Sargasso Sea, a strange dimension where lost things vanish to.

61

The idea of this super-sea was proposed by Charles Hoy Fort, writer and researcher into anomalous phenomena, with his tongue firmly in his cheek and in the spirit of the Greek sceptics. This, coupled with the concept of the 'mad fishmonger' was Fort's 'explanation' for the myriad reports of apparently terrestrial objects falling from the sky – like fish – and it can be extended to 'explanations' of UFO phenomena. It was Fort's way of ridiculing what he saw as the unimaginative tendency of the mainstream to 'explain things away' without actually investigating them fully, like the reports of rains of frogs and toads discounted as amphibians having been picked up by a tornado or whirlwind, without explaining why the wind picked up *just* frogs or toads.

This phenomenon of strange rains has been reported in some shape or form for hundreds of years, and there's still precious little information as to why they're so selective. Sometimes it's berries, sometimes it's fish, and sometimes of course, the classic frog falls. Fort's *Book of the Damned* (1919), *New Lands* (1923), and *Lo!* (1931)[2] record many of these reports of weird organic and apparently manufactured 'rain' from all over the world, with all sorts of interesting ingredients, including alabaster, ants, ashes, beef, beetle larvae, berries, bitumen, blood, butter, charcoal, china fragments (naturally vitrified?), cinders, coal, cobwebs, coins, crabs, crayfish, eels, fish, flesh, gelatinous matter, grain, hay, ice, iron balls, jellyfish, limestone, lizards, mud, mussels, oyster shells, periwinkles, quartz, resin, salt, sand, sandalwood, seeds, silk, snails, snakes, spawn, spiders, carved and shaped stones, turtles, and of course, toads and frogs. But never all at once, you understand.

Fort's sea idea was a satire on conventional explanations for such phenomena, and alludes to the Sargasso Sea of the Atlantic Ocean, which is tied into Bermuda Triangle myths, is known to be very salty, full of heavy drifts of seaweed, and is the breeding waters of the European and American eel. The Sargasso is known as the 'graveyard of ships' and even modern vessels can get their propellers snagged there, and end up drifting in its calm waters.

Back in 1997, I ended up expanding on Fort's idea for a crazy article called 'Super-Sargasso Surfin', which was published by *The*

Anomalist. This semi-satirical article is also published on Blather.net. In it, I speculated on how some reports of pre-twentieth-century UFOs, in the form of 'sailing ships' and 'mystery airships', were possibly connected to vessels sailing around in the Super Sargasso Sea.

My research at that time took me into notes written by James Hardiman in 1843 for Roderick O'Flaherty's *A Description of West or H-Iar Connaught* (1684), in a hunt for anomalous animal reports (and I can conclude that I found many, including mentions of Irish crocodiles). I stumbled across a note pertaining to the appearance of 'demon ships' in Galway Bay in 1161 AD, which was mentioned in the *Annals of the Four Masters*, a year-by-year history of Ireland from the 'earliest times' to 1616, compiled by four friars in the Abbey of Donegal in Bundrowes, on the coast near Bundoran.[3]

Fantastical Ships - Our annalists, in recording this occurrence, call these ships 'loinger demnacda' ...the meaning of demnacda, which literally signifies devilish or diabolical, from deaman (demon), the evil spirit. But our author's phrase, 'fantastical ships' (viz., visionary, or having the appearance of a phantom, not real), was happily chosen to express this instance of atmospheric refraction. [Ah, the wonders of science.] The writer remembers to have seen, when a boy, a well-defined aerial phenomenon of this kind, from a rising ground near the mountain of Cruach-Patrick [Croagh Patrick]. It was on a serene evening in the autumn of 1798. Hundreds who also witnessed the scene believed it supernatural; but it was soon afterwards found to have been caused by the fleet of Admiral Warren, then in pursuit of a French squadron, off the west coast of Ireland.

The Annals of the Four Masters holds other mentions of strange aerial vessels: 'Ships, with their crews, were plainly seen in the sky this year'. The year? AD 743.[4]

I unearthed other stories too. In 'Mystery Airships of the 1800s' in *Fate* magazine of June 1973, Jerome Clark and Loren Coleman wrote:

An ancient obscure Irish manuscript, *Speculum Regali*, records an incident that supposedly occurred in the year 956 AD: 'There happened in the borough of Cloera, one Sunday while people were at mass, a marvel. In this town there is a church to the memory of St. Kinarus. It befell that a metal anchor was dropped from the sky, with a rope attached to it, and one of the sharp flukes caught in the wooden arch above the church door. The people rushed out of the church and saw in the sky a ship with men on board, floating at the end of the anchor cable, and they saw a man leap overboard and pull himself down the cable to the anchor as if to unhook it. He appeared as if he were swimming in water. The folk rushed up and tried to seize him; but the bishop forbade the people to hold the man for fear it might kill him. The man was freed and hurried up the cable to the ship, where the crew cut the rope and the ship rose and sailed away out of sight. But the anchor is in the church as a testimony to this singular occurrence.'[5]

I began to wonder, with a smirk on my face, if an aerial wooden sailing ship could withstand the recoil of fully-loaded cannon? Could such a cannon propel a projectile through time and space into a mobile home in twentieth-century Missouri?

Soon after Blather.net's 'Smoking Cannon' article, folklorist Leslie Ellen Jones found the following on page eleven of Daibhí Ó Croinín's *Early Medieval Ireland 400-1200*:

The Annals of Ulster, for example, in the year AD 749 report that ships were seen in the air (some said above the monastery of Clonmacnois). Other sources report a similar episode at Teltown, during the reign of Congalach mac Maele Mithig (d. AD 956), when a ship appeared in the air above a market fair (oenach) and a member of the crew cast a spear down at a salmon below. When he came down to retrieve the spear a man on the ground took hold of him, whereupon the man from above said: 'Let me go! I'm being drowned!' Congalach ordered that the man be released and he scurried back up to his shipmates, 'who were all that time looking down, and were laughing together'. Well they might. There is no point in trying to explore the Otherworld with the apparatus and outlook of the science laboratory: flying ships are not subject to the laws of quantum mechanics. [6]

Then there's 'Magonia', a word that originates from a series of events, believed to have taken place in Lyons, France in around AD 833. Archbishop Agobard of Lyons[7] tells us that:

We have seen and heard from a lot of people so mad and blind as to believe and to assert that there exists a certain region called Magonia, from which ships, navigating on clouds, set sail to transport back to this same region the fruits of the earth ruined by hail and destroyed by storm, after the value of the wheat and the other fruits have been paid by these aerial navigators to the tempestarii, from whom they have received them. We have even seen several of these senseless fools who, believing the reality of such absurd things, brought in front of an assembly of men four persons in chairs, three men and a woman, who they said had fallen from these ships. They retained them in irons for some days, before they brought them before me, followed by the crowd, to stone them to death as they had been condemned, but after a long discussion, the truth finally triumphed after the many reasonings which I opposed to them and those who had shown them to the people were found, as a proverb has it, as much confused as a thief when he is surprised.

I should also add that in Gervase of Tilbury's *Otia Imperialis* from the thirteenth century, a very similar event is described as having taken place around AD 1200 at a church near Bristol.

Now this was all very well, all these arcane reports of medieval UFOs. But while it provided food for thought at the Blather Institute for Comedic Physics, it didn't explain the state of Leonard and Kathy Mickelson's mobile home. Still, we sat on the story, smug in our half-arsed pseudo-intellectual speculations and postulations. Until last year, some nine years later the cannonball story, I received an email from Kathy herself, who had found Blather.net after Googling herself. We exchanged a few emails, and then she sent me this report on what really happened:

> We do have an explanation as to who caused the damage and why he did it. He even had someone next door to us helping him to try to cover the noise. He used a homemade potato bomb as a projectile, trying to break into our home, in order to look for items to steal for drug money. He told this to the police, after the FBI and ATF were called in to canvass the neighborhood. They were searching up to a one-mile radius for a small Civil War-type cannon, like what would be used in a re-enactment or such. This individual was currently on probation for shooting a rifle at a school bus, interesting, wouldn't you agree? The St. Louis Post Dispatch did a story on it and they took film of a picture I had shot before the police had arrived, of the cannonball still in the wall behind our toilet. They were supposed to send it back, however I have never gotten it. The pictures I have now are of the damage, and there is a complete circle in two walls where you can look straight into the other room. There was around $13,000 worth of damage. Now that so much time has passed, I must tell you that it is an amusing life story. My husband is still called 'Cannonball' by certain friends at work.

So, there you have it. Sometimes maybe truth can be weirder than we imagine. There was nothing paranormal or anything in the realm of quantum physics going on in House Springs, Missouri: just some strange logic operating in the brain of nutty individual. Despite the media reports, it wasn't a cannonball at all, but a massive lump of potato, fired during a misguided attempt at breaking and entering.

But we can still dream of the Super-Sargasso Sea.

Dave Walsh

(Thanks to Kathy J. Mickelson for all her help.)

(1) Fortean list on yahoo.com: http://groups.yahoo.com/group/forteana/

(2) *Book of the Damned* ISBN 1-870870-53-0, *New Lands* ISBN 1-870870-62-x, *Lo!* ISBN 1-870870-89-1.

(3) *The Way That I Went*, Robert Lloyd Praeger, 1937. The Collins Press, ISBN 1-898-256-357.

(4) *Fortean Studies 2* ISBN 1-870-870-70-0 and Fortean Times 106:35.

(5) Interestingly, mention of the 956 A.D. incident is also mentioned in a United States Air Forces Academy textbook, *Introductory Space Science, Volume II*, Department of Physics, USAF, edited by Major Donald G. Carpenter and co-edited by Lt. Colonel Edward R. Therkelson. According to the online version, the book was taken off the curriculum in the 1970s, due of the controversy surrounding it.

(6) Daibhí Ó Croinin's *Early Medieval Ireland 400-1200* (Longman, 1995 ISBN: 0582015650). Leslie added that 'the actual text and translation of this episode is cited as being in Myles Dillon, 1960, 'Laud Misc. 610', *Celtica*, pp. 64-76, and Kuno Meyer, 1908, 'Irish mirabilia in the Norse *Speculum Regale*', *Eriu*, vol. 4, part 1, pp. 1-16.'

(7) Magonia: A Re-Evaluation, Jean Louis Brodu, Fortean Studies 2, ISBN 1-870870-70-0. The quotation is from Brodu's English translation from the French of Saint Agobard, De la Grêle et du tonnerre (Imprimerie de Dumoulin, Ronet et Sibuet, Lyons 1841), which is translated from the Latin of Archibishop Agobard of Lyons.

FEAR AND LOATHING
IN TELEMARK

It was 3 August 1998, and I was in Oslo's now-defunct Fornebu Airport, on my way to meet a monster, as one of twelve members of the grandly named GUST (Global Underwater Search Team), 130 kilometres west of Oslo in the county of Telemark. We were about to travel by mini-bus to Lake Seljord (*Seljordsvatnet*), to investigate 250 years of lake monster reports. I am not joking.

I'd been nervous about showing up. Don't get me wrong, it was an interesting proposition: invited to spend over two weeks in rural Norway, all expenses paid apart from flights, to research the biology and folklore surrounding a 200-year-old mystery. I imagined it as being a fairly multi-disciplinary project, unravelling the folkloric aspects of the legend, while biologist Jason Gibb would examine the lake's food chain. I wasn't clear on the roles of the other members, all of whom, curiously, were men, each of us with an interest in cryptozoology: the study of animals that are thought to exist, for which conclusive evidence is so far unavailable, and the study of known animals who are thought to be extinct, but have been the subject of contemporary sightings or reports.

I soon discovered that some of the others were unsure about the scheme. One member, Peter Lakbar, was apparently accused by the 'expedition' leader, Swedish cryptozoologist Jan-Ove Sundberg, of being a spy for a Swedish UFO magazine. I almost got kicked off the expedition because Jan thought I'd been 'too sceptical' in a *Sunday Business Post* interview. There was to be no alcohol consumed during the seventeen days; this was to ensure, according to

Jan, that we be taken seriously. We took it seriously alright: we just didn't drink when Jan was present.

Writing this nearly ten years later, I'm wondering what had me in Fornebu that day; probably a mix of curiosity, a taste for adventure and sheer devilment. I got more than I had bargained for; those two weeks in Seljord turned into one of the most hilarious farces I've ever been implicated in. I still get emails about it, especially when the associated documentary – shot for Discovery, Channel 4 and the BBC – gets another airing. A week after returning from Norway, I wrote about it on Blather.net and this is an update of that report. Back then, however, I had to be careful; the dust was too busy partying to consider settling down, legal threats were flying, and I had a website set up about me, claiming I was a Satanist and pornographer. In that blog, I didn't mention the really crazy stuff, like the narrowly-avoided fire engine theft, or the near riot in Seljord. I didn't tell about how the TV production started evolving into an *Apocalypse Now* sequel, how we endured the stink of catshit in our accommodation, or the apparently endless parade of snowball cocktails that we insisted on ordering in the leather-lined library of the local hotel.

Norway's countryside is *exactly* like those clichéd postcard images. For the first dozen kilometres to Lake Seljord I had my face out the van window, like a lobotomized Labrador, my ears flapping in the wind. By the time we got there my eyes were rolling and tongue lolling out, exhausted by the relentless beauty. The lake is a stunning fourteen-kilometre-long glacial cut in the mountains, about one kilometre wide and officially 138 metres deep.

The town of Seljord, at the top end of the lake, has adopted the Serpent as its coat-of-arms. It's an attractive, scattered community of 3,000 people, with one main drag of businesses. We were billeted at a beautiful farmhouse a few minutes out of town, and walking distance from the lake. The local council had mounted a tourism-driven campaign behind our monster project, and there was a lot of handshaking and photographs for the papers. Various technology companies showed up to sponsor us with equipment, including two different Simrad echo sounders, a side-scan sonar, a GPS hooked into a Konmap moving map system, and a couple of remote-control submarines. Jan definitely knew how to talk people into getting involved, myself included.

Jan put a huge emphasis on the equipment, mostly for the benefit of the media, who came in their dribs and drabs. We had a perfunctory lesson on the sounders and sonar, but using the submarines seemed premature; while there were anecdotal reports of underwater caverns in the lake, I thought it improbable that any anomalous creature would perform for the camera in the murky waters of the lake. During the two weeks, our one chance of sending a sub down to the deepest part of the lake had to be abandoned, due to heavy swells. As for our collective inexperience in using the other equipment, this led to disagreement later on. We all pretty much agreed that we were using it incorrectly, but there was little agreement on the nature of the misuse. This was not helped by problems with generators, and the regular breakdown of equipment.

With all this emphasis on mechanical toys, I began to wonder if my idea of what GUST was at all coincided with Jan's view. I arrived from Ireland thinking that we were going to examine the possibility of the Seljord monster being a real live known animal, or a new species (as unlikely as that would seem) and I took the view that if there was no such physical creature, then I'd still be interested in investigating the history and folklore. Jan, on the other hand, appeared to be convinced that the Norwegian Nessie existed in a literal, corporeal sense, and that it was simply a matter of us doing twenty-four-hour searches of the lake in order to find the damned thing. It wasn't clear exactly what he planned to do with it once he found it.

Jan split us into shifts, of four people each, that would spend eight hours out on the lake on board the home-made *Mother One*, built by Norwegian team member Arne Thomassen. Not to dismiss Arne's attempts, but *Mother One* was a little rickety. I wore my lifejacket when on board with Swedes Magnus Backlund and Peter Lakbar and Belgian Eric Joye; one can't be too careful. Magnus and Peter were easy to work with. But I found Eric to be a danger to shipping, and impossible to reason with. At one point he managed to drag *Mother One* across the top of the one set of submerged rocks we had been warned to avoid.

There were advantages. We were away from Jan, and being on day shift most of the time we could enjoy the scenery. For some reason, every bit of footage that the documentary team (who had a separate boat) got of me, I seem to be stuffing my face with food. We did actually put in a lot of effort, towing the sonar behind us, and watching the echo sounder for anything interesting. Magnus was on film talking about he should be at home taking care of his girlfriend and computer. I somehow got talked into reading aloud some passages from a book about monsters. In fairness, I couldn't blame Neil, the director, or the rest of the film crew. They were trying to make a viable movie out of what was rapidly descending into chaos and pseudoscience.

Out on the lake, we patrolled, and waited. Brief flurries broke out when interesting shapes showed up on the echo sounder traces. Two of the other team members, Ulf Burman and Peter Caspersson, saw 'something' from the road while driving. My notes read: '7 August 1998: 1140 sighting by Peter C and Ulf 75–100m north of Hugsdalen, momentarily seen thru trees from the road, partially obscured. 3m long black object breaking surface, not a wave. South–north alignment. Conditions, water choppy, SE wind, bright sunny day, with light cumulus clouds.'

We thought that this was an important sighting, regardless of what was the actual cause, as it demonstrated that odd things could be seen by drivers on the main road. Jan was vaguely interested for a while. In the meantime, Jason Gibb made some interesting bacterial finds while diving, leading to further speculation on the 'exploding log theory' (a 1985 article in *New Scientist* discussed theories of bacterial gasses on sunken logs in Scotland's Loch Ness: when the gases build to a high enough volume, the log rises to the surface briefly, before disappearing once again below the surface, giving rise to visions of Nessie).

Ulf Burman filmed lengthy footage of what he thought were live objects, moving just below the surface of the lake, leaving light 'v' wakes. Jason and Ulf's findings were more or less ignored by Jan. He was more enthusiastic about year-old reports from a local man of 'tracks': footprints in the silt twenty-five metres down. However, our scuba divers Jason and Kurt reported that the bottom was loose sediment, and any mark would be gone in a few hours. Jan still insisted that we go looking for the tracks.

In an email following the expedition he said, 'I think that the man fooled us, that the tracks were a practical joke that went too far,' and later that:

> I, Peter and other Swedes and also Arne sensed there was something wrong here and we did all we could to get our hands on [the witness], to have him show us exactly where the tracks were supposed to be. But the man avoided us at all costs, making up stories that he was on vacation, on the harvest, here and there and everywhere and at the end we just knew he was laying [*sic*] to us.

At the time, Jan's communication difficulties were not communicated to me, or anyone else that I was aware of. I did point out the uselessness of the information given to me by the witness over a telephone line, but was badgered instead by Jan for my scepticism.

The days wore on. After a spate of large echo soundings, some up to a couple of metres long, Jan was telling the press, and anyone who cared to listen, that we had had 'contact' with an object five metres long (the size fluctuated). I mightn't have had much experience with echo sounders, but at least some of us understood that echo sounders and sonar don't draw 2D pictures of 3D objects, they merely detect differences in density. They do not give any kind of conclusive evidence of the size or nature of an object.

A few days later, nearly two weeks into the trip, Jan suddenly claimed that he had taken photos of the monster. He told me that he was alone on the deck at the time, and didn't want to disturb the film crew, who were at work in the cabin. One would have thought that the prospect of filming a monster rising from depths of a lake would have had the film crew scrambling out onto the deck – but no, Jan kept it to himself, and didn't even mention it to other members of the team – who were on deck at the same time.

Afterwards, I heard a different version from the others on board, who maintained that Jan definitely wasn't on his own, and that what was seen and photographed was merely a series of waves or boat wakes. Nevertheless, Jan told us that he intended to sell the photos to UK paper *The Daily Express*, for the dubious sum of 60,000 Norwegian kroner (about €7,500). Before they were actually developed, Jan was planning to sell the alleged evidence of a creature only he had seen. On 13 August, he had Arne drive him to Oslo, where 'Kodak' developed the slides. I never did find out if it was *really* Kodak, or whether it was just a camera shop with a Kodak sign. On his return, he maintained that he had something very interesting to show us, which he did, in the form of an after-dinner slide show.

Unfortunately, where Jan could apparently see a 'serpent' in the photos, no one else could. A few people were saying 'well, maybe,' but both marine biologist Jason Gibb and I were quite vocal in our opinions that the photographs showed nothing other than, well, waves. We didn't rule out that Jan might have seen something, or that there was anything big and wriggly under the surface of the water, but we emphasized that, for us, the photographs displayed only waves. Jan insisted that 'Kodak' agreed with him about the photographs. 'When,' asked Jason, 'did Kodak become experts in nautical dynamics?'

A vote was called by Jan: who wanted to sell the photographs? There was a ten to two vote against. Jan said that he thought we'd like the money. It was pointed out that we didn't need it that badly. Jan replied that he would sell them for his own benefit anyway.

'What about the contract?' came a stunned question from the floor. 'Well, we can change the contract,' said Jan. We had signed an agreement that stated that any 'still photography, camcorder video and underwater video will, in the case of a sale to media or others, be shared equally between the team of twelve, which agrees to this'.

There was some laughter of disbelief. Obviously feeling cornered, Jan tried to put the team on a guilt trip by telling us that Arne had paid for boat fuel from his own pocket. According to Jan, we needed to sell the photos to cover the costs, or else pay 500kr (about €62) each. Jason said he would be happy to pay that amount, if it saved his integrity. I opined that the photos might show up in paranormal coffee table books for eternity, with our names attached. Pictures…of waves.

The meeting broke up; there was a definite rift in the camp. This, remember, was the evening of 13 August, and until the afternoon of Saturday 15, Jan not only sulked, but declined to speak English, and was rather curt to any of the Swedish or Norwegian people who didn't agree with him. We mulled the situation over snowballs, which turned into many snowballs. That somehow became a bottle of vodka at the local fire station, where we had access to the air pump for refilling scuba tanks. One geezer got a little out of control, starting the engines and sirens of the two fire engines, right in the middle of a small, otherwise silent town at 2am. After chasing him through the cabs of both trucks, we had to drag him by his legs and knock sense into him, before the local police arrived. They never did. In fact, the next day, no one even brought it up.

The whole expedition was getting far too silly. I was tired of the lack of proper research involved. Here we were, looking for a flesh and blood creature, without even a cursory glance at the local food chain. Jason and Kurt Burchfiel (a Boston policeman) were of the same thinking, and Jan's dismissive attitude towards any of our suggestions was starting to grate. The film crew was starting to flip out. Neil the director started seeing himself in Martin Sheen's Willard role from *Apocalypse Now*, with Jan as Brando's Kurtz. We were going up the lake…

One afternoon saw us using an Opel Corsa as a makeshift sound studio, with Neil the director, John the soundman and myself squashed inside. Neil was trying to persuade me to paraphrase from the movie, 'I think his methods are unsound'. The problem was that I didn't see any method at all, sir. Kurt appeared on a local radio show, and horrified the listenership with his deadpan criticism of junk he'd seen lying at the bottom of the lake. I can remember his voice suddenly coming on air while Jason and I were twiddling the radio knobs in a borrowed car. Kurt was in a phone box calling Boston, oblivious to the convulsion of laughter that we were in.

Kurt and I decided that we no longer wanted our names attached to the GUST circus. At a briefing on 15 August, we calmly gave our reasons, before leaving the room. Kurt explained how he felt that Jan had gathered together a bunch of genuine people and used them in his quest for money and notoriety. I finished off our resignation with how I had found it unacceptable that members of the team who were unable to speak Swedish or Norwegian had been cut from the information loop, when English was the official language of the expedition.

Afterwards, by email, Jan accused me of looking at him with 'cold, staring, murderous eyes' and having resigned in 'an aggressive manner'. The resignation was recorded for TV. I'd like to think that it shows me with blazing eyes, and Kurt and I smashing up furniture, but alas, we just said what we had to say, and left.

Kurt and I moved to the same hotel as the film crew. That night the chaos really kicked in. Neil locked himself in his room, evidently working on another Martin Sheen scene. The rest of the crew got ossified on moonshine at the local nightclub, a makeshift affair in the basement of the local fast food place, full of Norwegian teenagers. Out on the street, a fight nearly started after one English chap, ordinarily a totally professional type, suddenly became outrageously gay, upsetting some young blonde lad that he had his eye on. Following that, a caper involving bed sheets to smuggle local ladies into hotel rooms was thwarted by the eagle-eyed concierge, who'd already stopped them entering by the front door.

We spent the next day nursing hangovers, and winding up parts of the documentary that needed to be finished: so called 'perception tests', using floating logs. Jan, aboard *Mother One*, hung about offshore from where we were filming, taking photographs of us as, presumably as 'evidence'.

By the Monday, Kurt was on a flight back to Boston, and I was in Oslo, dragging myself through torrential rain, looking for decent accommodation and narrowly avoiding getting shacked up with a coterie of born-again Christians in an old warehouse. In the following days, I thought about the weird fortnight I'd been through. Jan may have only have been interested in money, notoriety etc., but I couldn't help thinking about a deeper, more mythological angle.

I had only recently read Patrick Harpur's wonderful book *Daimonic Reality*[1], in which he talks about the weird situation that prompted writer John Keel to write his book *The Mothman Prophecies*[2]:

> A quest, can perhaps be imagined as an extroverted version of the shaman's introversion – perhaps they are the outside and the inside of the same Way. Unlike the shaman, who is passive in the face of the dismembering otherworldly beings, the quester is active, single-minded, even obsessive. To draw mythological analogies, he is less like Orpheus, the archetypal shaman, than like Odysseus, Jason and Acneas, whose journeys took place through this world while beset at every turn by intrusions from the other. (In Christian terms, the quest becomes the pilgrimage while the shaman's journey becomes the mystic's ascent to God.) The danger for the shaman is that he might travel too far or too badly prepared into the Otherworld and so lose his soul; the danger for the quester is just the opposite – the Otherworld is too close to him, threatening to overwhelm and possess him. Even as he clings to his this-worldly perspective, which the shaman is compelled to give up, he is bombarded by the otherwordly. The song of the Siren lures him towards the mind-wrecking rocks. Paranoia is always just around the corner.

The more I thought about this, I began to consider Jan's project as a classic quest, in search of the Serpent, whatever it may be: the Nemesis of the quester perhaps, or the facing of one's demons? Even GUST's search plan had a heading, *The Search for the Serpent*.

Jan confirmed this in an email after the expedition, writing 'internally we were talking about the serpent or the serpents but to the media I said we weren't sure there was unknown animals in the lake.'

Brewer's Dictionary of Phrase and Fable, under the heading of 'Serpent', says that 'In Scandinavian myth, the Nidhogg, the Dread Biter, is evil as living at the root of the Yggdrasil and trying to destroy it' (the Yggdrasil is the 'world-tree', the connection between heaven and earth, and it is 'the tree of life and knowledge, and of time itself').

Under the heading of the Old Serpent, Brewer writes: 'And he laid hold on the dragon, that old serpent, which is the Devil, and Satan, and bound him a thousand years. Revelations XX,2'.

If I am right, and Jan was on bit of a 'serpent quest', it's rather ironic that following the GUST debacle, he accused me of Satanism. This was my perceived scepticism, my references to being an occasional 'devil's advocate' when during discussions, my very occasional habit of signing myself off in Irish, i.e. 'is mise le meas' ('yours respectfully'), with Daithí Breathnach, the Gaelic form of my name. Jan wondered if I was 'speaking in tongues' and whether I'd changed my name for membership of a 'satanic sect'.

I was tossing around serpentine ideas in my head on 18 August, in Oslo's Vigeland Park, designed by sculptor Gustav Vigeland. 'Guarding' the park's bridge were four pillars, each topped with a sculpture of a person being savaged by some form of weird beast, in three cases serpent-like creatures. Old Gustav seemed to have a whole primeval Human versus the Serpent thing going on, as depicted throughout a considerable amount of his sculpture, and also his metalwork, as evinced by the Park gates. Vigeland figured out how to externalize his demons, it seems.

Back in Ireland, the GUST fall-out continued. Jan sent me an email, telling me that he was exposing me on a website. I had a look, and then forwarded it to friends. It was called 'Dave Walsh is the Right Hand of the Devil' and referred to the supposedly satanic behaviour

mentioned above. He contacted the employers of another partici-
pant, who apparently almost lost his job over allegations made by Jan.
I'm told that the production company, who made the documentary,
Cicada, was harassed by threatening phone calls.

Despite all of the weirdness, I had a great time. It was a charac-
ter-building exercise, and it definitely left me more equipped for
dealing with bullshit, and with a much thicker neck for fending
off insults.

I'm only sorry that those few weeks in Norway didn't involve
a serious study of Lake Seljord. Unfortunately, witness reports and
anecdotes were regarded as unquestioned fact, when there are huge
coatings of recurring motifs and myths which need to be stripped
from lake monster reports before anything useful can be derived.
Harpur writes the following about Michel Meurger's book *Lake
Monster Traditions*[3]:

> In the case of lake monsters, Meurger established that the following
> motifs – he calls them 'folklore beliefs' – are pretty much universal.
> Beginning with the lake itself, it is bottomless; it interconnects with
> other lakes or the sea; it is the scene of anomalous luminous phenom-
> ena; it is impenetrably dark; it has submarine caverns; it has strong
> currents and eddies or whirlpools which are caused by (or sometimes
> synonymous with) serpents; it is prone to unexpected squalls; it has
> swallowed up divers who never return.

Until these recurring motifs are weeded out (but not completely
discarded, as they may indeed be some truth in them – a lake may
have some of the properties described, but they aren't necessarily
proof of anything), then a real investigation of a lake monster report
cannot be taken seriously, except perhaps as a study of modern
folklore. Worse still, if the organizers of questionable, chaotic projects
like GUST can't even decide whether they're hunting monsters or
conducting an investigation, then the issue will remain mired in the
realm of pseudo-science forever.

'I watched a snail crawl along the edge of a straight razor. That's my dream. That's my nightmare. Crawling, slithering, along the edge of a straight... razor... and surviving' – Kurtz, *Apocalypse Now*.

Dave Walsh

(1) Patrick Harpur, *Daemonic Reality* (Penguin, ISBN 0-14-019-485-1).
(2) John Keel, *The Mothman Prophecies* (Tor Books, 0765341972).
(3) Michel Meurger, *Lake Monster Traditions* (Fortean Tomes 199, ISBN 1-870021-00-2).

MAYDAY!

Late at night, somewhere in Ireland, a shadowy figure will be crossing the land. He or she will be holding in their hand a bag, or a box of eggs. They might bend to dig and bury an egg in a field, or, creeping closer to an outhouse, lay one gently inside some straw or hay. The moon will be almost full, so the light is good, and the ground dry. It is a good night to be out in the fields with malice in your heart…

This night is May Eve, the night before 1 May, the feast of Bealtaine, also known as Mayday. This is an old Celtic feast day that marked the start of summer, the day when cattle were driven out to pasture. Bealtaine is calculated as a quarter day, between the Vernal equinox on 21 March and Midsummer Solstice on 21 June. This actually makes the real Bealtaine fall between 5 and 7 May.

This festival that welcomes summer has some darker moments before the sun rises. This is the night for making a pisheog, a kind of Irish curse. Pisheogs are made to bring ill health or ill wealth to your neighbours. My mother told me about a neighbourhood man who made pisheogs when she was a child in Craughwell, a village in east County Galway. Her family kept a small farm in the locality. On May Eve she and her sisters would be sent out, bottle of holy water in hand, to 'bless the fields' and keep them safe against pisheogs. She told me how everyone in the village knew the man who cast them, yet no-one would move to stop him. She would watch to see him going down the road with his horse in the dark of night, on his way to wander through their fields to bury eggs in the land. The egg was buried with the intention of making the ground 'go sour', while one left in a barn or outhouse was to make the milk of a cow dry up, or to stop butter from being produced in the churn.

Another custom concerning butter was that anything stolen from around a farm on May Day would 'steal the butter' from the house. This meant that the victim's churn wouldn't produce any butter and the 'thief' would benefit from added wealth. Churning itself was mostly avoided on Bealtaine, unless a drop of holy water was added. No fire was allowed to leave the house, so any man smoking had to smoke his pipe within the walls. If he left with the pipe lit, it was feared that the luck of the house would leave with it, and this would affect the butter. If all precautions had been made, and the butter still wasn't appearing during churning, then it was suspected that evildoing and pisheogs were to blame. The cure for this was to plunge a red-hot tongs deep into the churn to burn away the evil.

Near where I've been living, close to the villages of Ennistymon and Lahinch in County Clare, you can see branches left, or tied outside doors to protect against the pisheog. They must be left by another neighbour however, not yourself. I've noticed that the branches I've seen left are horse chestnut, but I'm not sure if this tree is the only one used in this custom.

The May Bush is another custom of the first of May. A tree, usually a rowan (mountain ash) or hawthorn, is decorated with cloths, ribbons and egg shells. This welcomes in the summer as well as warning off bad luck.

In ancient times, bonfires were lit on high ground across the country, especially on County Westmeath's Hill of Uisneach, known as the 'Navel of Ireland', an important spiritual and political centre. This custom has died out in most areas, but still continues in parts of Galway and Limerick.

There are also some first of May traditions related to the Virgin Mary. At the foot of the Paps Mountains in County Kerry there is a holy well sacred to her. The well sits in an old fort called Cathair Crobh Dearg. On the Sunday closest to Mayday, rosaries are said in a clockwise direction around the fort. Incidentally, the Paps

Mountains are said to be the breasts of Danu, an ancient Munster goddess.

In the 1973 cult horror film *The Wicker Man*, the plot centres on a celebration of Mayday. A police officer, played by Edward Woodward, is unwittingly lured to an island in Scotland where the 'old religion' still flourishes. As the plot unfolds, many old Mayday customs are illustrated, including children dancing around the Maypole. The island's inhabitants, however, have much darker things in mind for their guest.

While some of the May customs of pisheogs and May bushes have died out, you can still find evidence of them continuing, in particular around County Clare. Especially around my house…

Suzanne Walsh

NORWAY'S PSYCHIC PRINCESS

Princess Märtha Louise (b.1971), fourth in line to the Norwegian throne, has declared 'I am psychic' and is opening a school to teach people how to communicate with angels. The Princess has been in contact with winged celestials, having previously had her third eye opened by communicating telepathically with horses.

Märtha Louise, whose tax returns for 2006, according to the newspaper *Dagbladet*, show net assets of over six million Norwegian kroner (about €750,000), is setting up the school with Elisabeth Samnøy, a thirty-nine-year-old former assistant ships' mechanic, who registered assets of zero (her surname the papers have also spelled 'Sømnøy', but not 'Rasputin'). The school is called Astarte Education, named after Astarte, goddess of fertility, sexuality and war. Fertility is mentioned on their website but there's no mention of sex and violence. Interestingly, the horse is one of Astarte's symbols; the fact that this does not warrant a mention, as it should, may indicate the Princess doesn't know.

The unaccredited three-year course presents a programme in which the first year focuses on (energy) readings, the other on healing and the third on (angel) contacting. That costs 24,000 kroner a year (about €3,000). The psychic duo writes:

> Through meditation and self-development you can come in contact with the true you... [You will start to] live from your own strength and your essence. When you do that, your life changes from a life lived out from others' point of view, to becoming a life that is created

such as you will have it. [My translation.]

Communication with angels will apparently help this development.

The Princess seems to have always been headed in this direction, or at least interprets her previous life this way now. She has this magical memory of her childhood:

I remember particularly one time I met a foreign lady when I was little. I went over to her and said that she didn't need to be sorry for her man, it will be well. The woman dropped her chin in disbelief and wondered who it was who had told me about her. It became a big commotion. [My translation.]

A horse rider at competition level, Märtha Louise has said in the past that she wordlessly communicates with horses, but she has also said it is good that horses take her as she is, and are unoccupied with her status as royalty. Perhaps this is a telling point.

I note a contradiction in what Märtha Louise and Elisabeth are offering. By believing that there is a 'true' self, one is denying the notion of free will. If one has a true self, it is one's innate nature and therefore there is nothing one can do to change it. Yet they are offering change, towards life as 'you will have it', i.e. freely chosen. The self-created individual and the innate 'true' self are irreconcilable opposites. But maybe this really has nothing to do with the make-up of the self in any kind of philosophical sense. Let's imagine for example you are a princess, raised with a defined role, feeling like you're living your life from others' point of view. You have felt since childhood that this perhaps was not the 'real' you. When you get to your mid-thirties, you might be inclined to finally cast off that imposed role and do what you have wanted to do all along? Like express something wild, esoteric, imaginative?

Why is it that people with 24,000 kroner to burn a year are not living life as they would have it? What is it that needs 'healing'? Now, I may be just a speck of dust on the grimy windscreen of the universe, knowing more about dead flies than angels, but I'm of a similar age to the Princess, and speaking from my own personal experience here, I have no money at all, but do more or less what I want to do in life. Perhaps there is an inverse relation between wealth and freedom, and in the absurd world of royalty, this disharmony is accentuated.

But I don't want to leave this subject without mentioning what the reaction to her opening an angel communication school has been like in Norway.

Clifford Pickover, in his book *The Girl Who Gave Birth To Rabbits* (about Mary Toft, the woman who faked giving birth to a litter of rabbits in 1726), didn't see much difference between the delusions of the eighteenth century and our age, and he wrote,

> What I have learned from Mary's legacy is that there is increasing urgency for scientists and leaders to be vigilant in their struggle against hoaxes, especially now that the mass media make it particularly difficult to distinguish fact from fiction... Nonscientific reasoning and bizarre therapies are gaining acceptance as medical treatments... The best way of battling the spread of pseudoscience is an enlightened public, able to distinguish logic from delusion, charlatans from truth-tellers.

Within this context, it can be seen that for some people, a school that teaches people to communicate with angels is, in a sense, a threat. And on 31 July 2007 Trygve Hegnar, a writer in the financial newspaper *Finansavisen*, labelled Märtha as nothing more than a swindler. His view was that her school's promises are in conflict with marketing laws. In the cultural newspaper *Morgenbladet,* Carl-Erik Grimstad warned thinking people and democrats against the blending of monarchy with religion, referring to royals in Europe's distant past who were said to have magical healing hands.

The Princess got no support either from Christian quarters. The Christian politician Inge Lønning's position was that the teachings of the angel school are 'on a collision course with Christian belief,' as the tabloid *VG* put it. Lønning said to the newspaper *Aftenposten*, 'the religion... prevailing in Norway before Christianity... was a belief in one's own power... These notions can't combine with a Christian belief in God.'

Märtha obviously did not ignore these criticisms, and became sick, cancelling two weeks of engagements, because of the hullaba-loo surrounding the angel school.

Princess Märtha Louise's first official engagement since the 'angel-noise' (*VG*'s phrase!) was the Bislett Summer Games on 11 August. Amusingly, Geir Smeby of the Games told the internet newspaper *Nettavisen* that questions about the angel school were forbidden. 'We decline to lose focus on our event to the benefit of angels. Such questions are not acceptable,' he said.

There has of course been support for the Princess. Her sister-in-law Mette-Marit, the 'commoner' who married the Crown Prince and became staple tabloid-fodder, declared in *Dagbladet* on 27 July that she 'was healed by Märtha'. Yes, 'when the Crown Princess Mette-Marit had a kidney infection, she was treated by her psychic sister-in-law's warm hands.'

Then on the night of 2 August there was Irish support, in the form of middle-aged singer Sinead O'Connor, who was in Trondheim for a concert. Translated back into English from Norwegian, Sinead's words of support were: 'All have their own theories. I believe in angels, maybe they are everywhere but we can't see them the whole time.' But O'Connor didn't stop there, and went on to say that she has a friend who believes clouds are angels. Not stopping there either, she then revealed that she herself has met angels: 'I am of the understanding that angels can take up residence in human beings, and I have myself met people who I later have understood are angels'. What does Märtha Louise make of *that*?

The Princess finally opened the angel school, and the teaching began in August, but alas, without a location for the school. So I can't go there to tell you what it's like.

The address for the school (for now) is apparently the Princess' home address in Lommedalen. There has been this announcement on the Astarte Education website. [My translation.]

> We at Astarte Education know that there is a location for the course that awaits us. It just hasn't found us yet. If you know about a place for sale, preferably an apartment that is regulated for business activity with a big room that can fit 30 people and 3 small rooms that can be used for individual treatment sessions, that has a little kitchen, wooden floor, preferably with a fireplace, a lot of light and a nice backyard, situated in central Oslo, we are interested.

So imagine something like that. And Märtha Louise, Elisabeth, the angels, their followers, and you.

Barry Kavanagh

THE 9/11 CONSPIRACY THEORIES

THE CALL TO ADVENTURE

I've been avoiding the 9/11 issue, if the truth be told, for a long time now. I started dabbling with the 9/11 conspiracy theories a few months back by listening to podcasts, reading articles and yes, watching the movie *Loose Change*, the amateur-made film on 9/11 which sits at the very centre of most of the recent conspiracy theories.

Whilst you have to admire the ingenuity of those responsible for the movie, you also feel forced to point out that this is, for some, a movie so patently ridiculous in its claims, so hysterical in its tone, so desperate to find evidence to fit its theory, that one exasperated blogger recently likened watching it to being 'bukakked with stupid'. However, George Monbiot writing in to *The Guardian* in February 2007, articulates the issues a bit better:

> To qualify as a true opponent of the Bush regime, you must also now believe that it [the Bush regime] is capable of magic. It could blast the Pentagon with a cruise missile while persuading hundreds of onlookers that they saw a plane. It could wire every floor of the twin towers with explosives without attracting attention and prime the charges (though planes had ploughed through the middle of the sequence) to drop each tower in a perfectly timed collapse. It could make Flight 93 disappear into thin air, and somehow ensure that the relatives of the passengers collaborated with the deception. It could recruit tens of thousands of conspirators to participate in these great crimes and induce them all to have kept their mouths shut, for ever.

REFUSAL OF THE CALL

Now, wait. Calm down. Take a deep breath. Before we get ourselves dragged back into yet more arguments about 'what plane did what at what time', I'd like to suggest that an issue far worthier of discussion is the basic matter of *why* these conspiracy theories exist at all. Why has there been such a ground-swell of almost religious fervour which demands that we now accept 9/11 was an inside job? What do these stories do? What's their function?

SUPERNATURAL AID

The makers of *Loose Change* see shadowy government agents at every turn. 'They' haunt almost every utterance and nothing is ordinary. Everything is extraordinary. But there's nothing there. I'm sorry, there just isn't. There's nothing. No evidence. No documents. No learned testimony. No verifiable facts. And whilst would-be Forteans such as ourselves here at Blather.net are supposed to remain impartial and seek a condition of 'negative capability', there are occasions when the sheer critical mass of acceptable stupidity and the ease with which so many are buying into this half-assed, hysterical, unverifiable conjecture as though it were fact, simply becomes too much to bear. And, it is no different when it comes to 9/11.

CROSSING THE FIRST THRESHOLD

Now, conspiracy theories and theorists fascinate me. They're usually passionate, articulate and persuasive people. Their devotion to their studies brings out that most wonderful of human qualities which Ian Fleming described (in the novel *Goldfinger*) as the singular joy of being taught a new subject by an expert in that field. I'm also fascinated by the belief-systems at work: the 'storytelling' that goes into creating a conspiracy and what we can learn about ourselves by looking at the mechanics of that story. Many suggest that the words we use shape the way we see the world. And conspiracy theory, whether genuine investigative journalism or cheap text-polls, creates quite a world.

THE BELLY OF THE WHALE

For me though, the only 'truth' in all of this, is that conspiracy theorists are searching for meaning in chaos. The problem is that sometimes, there is no meaning. There's just chaos. Meteorites fall from the sky every day. People get cancer. Bad shit happens. *All* the time.

THE ROAD OF TRIALS

Sometimes there's just madness. And there's nothing you can do about it. Elvis left the building a long time ago. That UFO you saw? Be honest, it was *probably* a Chinese *Kongming* lantern. For me the insistence that we have no free choice, that every event in our lives is dictated by a nefarious, unseen cabal of Illuminati, is in itself the ultimate fascism: the rabid, never-ending insistence that we have no choice. The 'you're with us or against us' rhetoric is remarkably similar to that of the regime which it seeks to criticize.

Some, in their quasi-messianic zeal to prove that Bush and the neocons orchestrated 9/11, have done such a good job of convincing their audience of the sheer scale of the conspiracy, that they have done a rather excellent job of convincing them of their political impotence.

THE MEETING WITH THE GODDESS

Our world needs no Illuminati. It needs no saucer-people who live below the polar caps. It needs no race of super-human, blood-drinking mole-people to govern us like serfs. We have the UN Security Council to do that for us. You want to investigate something? Get over to Greg Palast's website and investigate how it is that the Republicans stole an entire election. Find out where the Enron money went. Ask why it is that the Japanese government are hell-bent on killing over 900 whales for 'scientific study'.

TEMPTATION AWAY FROM THE TRUE PATH

Sometimes, it seems that when something horrible happens to a nation, people, naturally, search for meaning in it. Quite frequently there isn't any. Michael Collins was assassinated in 1922, in Béal na mBláth in Ireland and people are still speculating as to who shot him. Diana died ten years ago because she slammed into a wall at over 100 miles per hour. Not because of some vast Masonic conspiracy. Katrina was a hurricane. Not a Tesla weapon.

ATONEMENT WITH THE FATHER

America has no cultural experience of this. No lens through which to understand events such as this. Having never been invaded or carpet-bombed, never suffered the real ravages of terrorism and having exported its war across the globe, many citizens of the United States are bereft of the 'language' with which they can make sense of the sheer scale of what 9/11 was.

And perhaps, ultimately the real problem is just that: the sheer scale of the event. It was so spectacular, so 'Hollywood movie', that almost immediately people start rooting around for the 24-like grand-plan, when in actual fact it's far more likely that 9/11 was the result of the work of a bunch of evil, scheming religious zealots who despise America and every thing that it stands for. There's nowhere near as many of them as you've been told there is and they ain't that hard to find: just go to the poorest places on earth.

APOTHEOSIS

Now don't get me wrong: I am under no illusion as to what kind of people Bush, Cheney, Rumsfeld and the rest of that shower are. Yes, 9/11 helped them. Yes, it was convenient. But only because the people of America allowed it to be so. It was not engineered by the CIA or even by Bin Laden, or indeed by the 'Project for a New American Century'. It was organized by a loosely-connected group of religious fundamentalists, the majority of whom all came from one of America's closest 'allies'. Ask about *that* before you start screaming for Iran's invasion.

THE ULTIMATE BOON

It's time to up the game. Time to get better. Time to write better blogs, make better movies and ask better questions. I'm sorry, but *Loose Change* and the 9/11 conspiracy theorists are just not doing that right now. Yes, there are aspects of 9/11 that are troubling. The twenty-eight missing pages from the joint congressional committee's report on 9/11 are a serious issue. But to buy in completely, well, let me go back to Monbiot:

> In other words, you must believe that Bush, Cheney, Rumsfeld and their pals are all-knowing, all-seeing and all-powerful, despite the fact that they were incapable of faking either weapons of mass destruction or any evidence at Ground Zero that Saddam Hussein was responsible. You must believe that the impression of cackhandedness and incompetence they have managed to project since taking office is a front. Otherwise you are a traitor and a spy.

Damien DeBarra

SUPERSTITIONS OF CHRISTMAS

Most people associate Christmas with the pleasure of giving gifts, or the enjoyable tradition of drinking oneself stupid. But this time of celebration is also associated with other, far weirder customs. If you wish to avoid bad luck in the coming year, you would do well to be cautious. For example, ivy and holly, seemingly innocent decorations that we place in our homes, have certain superstitions surrounding them.

Ivy has something of a mixed reputation in both Ireland and England. A plant of ill omen, it should not be used alone or overused when decorating the house for Christmas. Although regarded as bad luck, it was also thought of as a plant of divination. In Cornwall there is a saying, 'Anyone who wishes to dream of the devil should pin four ivy-leaves to the corner of his pillow.'

As for holly, it can be taken as good luck when a sprig of Christmas holly is thrown on the fire and makes a crackling sound. But if it burns with a dull flame and makes no sound, there could be a death in the family within the year. Such beliefs were widespread in nineteenth and twentieth-century Britain and Ireland. Holly is a tree with lots of customs. For instance, like a faery tree, it should not be cut down. In mid-twentieth-century Devon this was the case: 'About fifteen years ago two holly trees were cut down in the parish. Locals protested violently, saying this would produce poltergeist havoc.'

Nowadays, to avoid bad luck, we know to take the decorations down by the twelfth day of Christmas. In the early twentieth century, decorations were left up till Candlemas Day, the second of February. A quote from Worcestershire explains, 'It is unlucky to keep Christmas holly about the house after Candlemas Day, as the Evil One will then come himself and pull it down.' In Suffolk in 1864 it is recorded that 'If every scrap of Christmas decoration is not removed from the church before Candlemas Day there will be a death within a year in the family occupying the pew where a leaf or berry is left.'

The apparently innocuous mince pie also has strange superstitions attached, such as this one from late nineteenth and twentieth-century England: 'Mince pies, too, have their own magic; if you eat twelve of them, from twelve separate friends, during the twelve days of Christmas, you are promised a lucky twelve months to follow.' This may be an excuse for gluttony. It is also reportedly bad luck to eat mince pies outside of the twelve days of Christmas.

Another strange belief is associated with Christmas Eve. 'At midnight on Christmas Eve cattle are supposed to kneel in their stalls in adoration of the Saviour. It is said that anyone who enters the stable to test this, will be struck dead.' This is from 1927 England. My mother grew up in rural east Galway in the 1950s. She has a different memory of Christmas Eve: 'Whenever my father or farmers in the locality went to check on their animals, at the time of night when Jesus was born, the animals would be kneeling down.' She remembers another belief associated with New Year:

> Every sixth of January the family, including extended family, would gather to say the rosary. Before we started it was traditional to light little candles. We had a board, and we'd each stick a candle to the board. Everyone had their own colour. The candles would be lighting all through the rosary, and as they were burning, the children would build up the candle grease to made their candle last, as the tradition was that whoever's candle died first, they would be the first to die.

Another important date until recently was Holy Innocents' Day, 28 December. This is the day dedicated to the first-born children slaughtered by Herod (Matthew 2:1-18). This day is also known as Childermas. It was known as a 'dismal' day, a day that was unlucky.

Despite falling within the twelve days of Christmas it was known be a heavy and subdued day. In the Aran Islands fishermen refused to leave the harbour to fish. If anything was started on this day, it was sure to go wrong. Washing yourself or clothes was avoided as this could cause a death in the family. Melton says in 1620, observing Cornish superstitions of that day, 'that it is not good to put on a new sute, pare ones nailes, or begin any thing on a Childermas day'. Donkeys fared a little better from this day of hardship. They were given a day of rest and an extra feed, in thanks for helping Mary's flight to safety in Egypt. If not observed the ubiquitous bad luck will be sure to follow.

Another animal to do well at Christmas is the fly. Try not to harass or kill them and they will bring you good luck. Even if they are licking your dinner.

A final word concerns gifts. Even this harmless custom could incur doom: 'A small Herefordshire farmer sometime since made lamentations, that a pair of new shoes had been unwittingly received into his house on Christmas morning, and said it was "bad job" for he "lost a sight of cattle that year."'

If there is anything to be learned, it is to be a little cautious around Christmas, as the year ahead, or indeed life, could depend on it.

Suzanne Walsh

THE ANTHROPOLOGY
OF ROADS

My anthropological study of roads emerged from my observation that motorists and pedestrians seem to ignore the existence of cyclists, as if they are not really present with them on the routeways they traverse.

Of course, this led me to suspect that much is going on at the subconscious level, where cyclists are being 'filtered out'. It was also quite telling that when motorists and pedestrians do seem to notice cyclists, it is to engage in violent altercations with them.

The invention of the bicycle in 1861 represents the beginning of the modern era. Those who remained pedestrians after this watershed moment represent a backwards-looking and resentful tendency that has greeted modernity. Fear of technology, and a belief that everything was better in the past, has given rise to the pedestrian of today. It is notable that even though the noun 'pedestrian' is neutral in meaning, the adjective 'pedestrian' is exclusively pejorative. However, the pedestrians have been, in some sense, right to fear technology. Motorists, in the ascendant since the invention of the automobile in 1885, represent an extreme of modernity, that anti-human and antisocial tendency that threatens society.

In the motorist, we observe major psychological dysfunctions emerging from the ego.

Motorists are egotistical. Hence, the ego manifestation boxes ('cars') in which they propel themselves about the planetary landscape. A car is always physically larger than the motorist's own (human) body, as it is the physical manifestation of the ego that has inflated beyond the physical space the body occupies. Motorists will not always be aware of their ego problem, subconsciously inventing the 'need' for a car, such as the placement of their habitat ('home') far away from the place where they must forage ('work').

Motorists are antisocial. Their immersion in their own egos results in a loss of interest in society. They are happy for people to be kept at a distance from one another, as they see interaction as mere ego-clash. Their own egos are so inflated that they see all egos as equally in need of ostentatious physical manifestation. Motorism promotes the redesign of towns, cities, countryside, and the planet in general to meet the needs of the car. In essence, the motorist wishes to replace the presence of interactive human society on the streets and greens with the constant traffic of machines. The car is thus more than an ego manifestation box: it also has an antisocial function, separating people from one another.

Motorists are subconsciously homicidal. If you are egotistical and antisocial, the next logical step is obviously going to be the desire to kill other human beings. The reason the car is so fast, and so heavily armoured, is to satisfy this subconscious urge to kill. The homicidal impulse is indulged with car ownership, which is the attainment of the power to kill. This feeling of power can be enough to keep the homicidal impulse tamed, but motorists find it difficult not to desire 'accidents', in which their urge to kill is finally sated. Motorists will always claim that cycling is 'dangerous', because they want to be able to murder cyclists with impunity, by making it look like the cyclists' 'fault'. But cycling is not inherently dangerous. Cyclists are only in danger from those people who profess it to be dangerous, i.e. those who deliberately wish to make it so.

The pedestrian leads generally a more positive existence than that of the motorist. The pedestrian is, after all, out in society interacting with other human beings, without the distancing effect of metal armour. But pedestrians are seriously psychologically dysfunctional, and these dysfunctions stem from their self-loathing. Unlike the rampantly egotistical motorist, the pedestrian suffers from a lack of ego. Pedestrians hate themselves, and that is why they don't cycle. This is the explanation for their rejection of the bicycle's invention in 1861: their self-hatred disallowed their participation in the elevation of quality of life that the bicycle represented. Pedestrians know cycling would be good for their health, yet they don't cycle, taking perverse pleasure instead in their psycho-physical deterioration. They know too that cycling will save them the money they would otherwise waste on public transport, yet they don't cycle: in fact, they will often choose a habitat at an awkward location in relation to their 'work', which guarantees them the necessity to use the most unpleasant form of public transport, as they enjoy being miserable, packed in like sardines with other miserablists. For many of these ego-depleted self-loathing individuals, ego-compensation can only be achieved through escape into the sickness of car purchase, which is, of course, over-compensation and leads to egotism and the other psychological dysfunctions of the motorist.

As I noted above, the pedestrian is not antisocial in the way that motorists are. But the pedestrian is antisocial in relation to the cyclist. The cyclist represents to pedestrians the symbol of everything a pedestrian could be: healthy, sane, thrifty etc. and this causes deep resentment. The pedestrian wishes to physically attack a cyclist, so will subconsciously filter out all visual and aural information relating to cyclists, only 'noticing' the cyclist in an 'accident', or near-'accident' situation. The more desperately aggressive pedestrians will 'notice' cyclists at traffic lights, zebra crossings or in parks, and will hope for some kind of altercation. Unlike the motorist, however, the pedestrian is not homicidal. Rather, the pedestrian prefers to enact beatings and maimings, and does not require the need for the certainty of killing power (unless, of course, the pedestrian goes on to become a motorist). The archetype of the pedestrian is the street thug. Pedestrians, if they are not already in a street gang, are sad, frustrated people itching to join one.

It seems to me that cyclists represents the 'norm' in terms of healthy human psychology, and they exist in a dysfunctional society, sandwiched in between two frighteningly dysfunctional groups, motorists and pedestrians.

Dr Stewart Roberts

CLONTARF-BASED SCIENCE TEAM FIND 'THE CLITORIS'

(From the archives: an investigative report from Blather News®)

A team of elite adventurers, maverick scientists and fornicating bloggers have shocked the scientific community today with a breathtaking announcement. 'After almost two millennia of fruitless searching' said Professor Jim-Bob Gobstopper, 'it would appear that we have done the unthinkable. We can reveal the secret of *how to find the clitoris.*'

The announcement has been greeted with shock, excitement and outrage by Dublin scientists, politicians and prostitutes. Professor Gobstopper, joined by a phalanx of white-coated colleagues, held a press conference at Dublin Castle this morning to elaborate on his findings. Blather.net dispatched its award-winning Science/Celebrity/Vaginal Surgery correspondent, Filthy Hack, to get the scoop. When vigorously cross-examined on the validity of this astonishing claim, Gobstopper showed the thronging crowd of assembled scientists, saddlesniffers and pornographers some intriguing footage, filmed, it would appear, on a mobile phone. After some unintentional amusement (when the Professor accidentally showed a video clip of one of his interns happy-slapping a sheep), the gathering were treated to an exclusive look.

The footage, later uploaded to Youtube (causing the site to temporarily crash), revealed a small, bleary-eyed pink object. Gobstopper explained that over-exposure to bright lights is deeply damaging to the creature and that the film had to be shot in low-light to save it from injury.

Gobstopper elaborated on the intriguing and revolutionary process by which he and his team conducted their research. Using EU grants to the tune of €8 billion, Gobstopper and his team hired an army of prostitutes, gathered from the four corners of the European Union, to assist in the world's largest synchronized vaginal-prodding. The entire event was filmed by a battery of two thousand hi-def digital cameras on loan from George Lucas. A highlights package is mooted for a Christmas DVD release. The clip shown at the conference, Gobstopper claimed, showed 'merely the tip of the big pink iceberg'.

Almost immediately, the film footage became the source of controversy. 'The film was a touch fuzzy and the sound was slightly obscured by a loud seventies wah-wah-pedal guitar soundtrack, but it would, at first glance, appear to be genuine,' said an Irish Government spokesman, Senator Keith Gill.

The revelation has astounded scientists across the globe. 'I mean seriously now, this is breathtaking stuff. A discovery on a par with Crick and Watson's double helix,' said Dr Brian Redmond of the Los Angeles Institute of Vaginal Mythology. Others were not so impressed.

Leading proctologist Ian Devine threw doubt on the claims. 'You must understand, this claim is quite incredible. Over two and a half thousand years of medical history and suddenly it turns up in the back of a Fiat Punto on Dollymount Strand? I don't fucking think so. Next he'll be announcing he's found the G-spot. Pfff .'

We called the offices of Professor Gobstopper in Clontarf, Dublin for an interview but his office was, according to his secretary, currently besieged by a horde of rampaging housewives. More as we get it.

Damien DeBarra

ANCIENT IRISH ASTRONAUTS

Over the years, much spite and spittle has been spent in Dublin pubs and letters' pages about the Spire of Dublin, the Monument of Light, known to every sleeveen or corner boy as 'De Spike' or the 'Stiffy by the Liffey'. It's a wondrous thing altogether, commissioned for the millennium celebrations in memory of the city's heroin addicts, and it arrived bang on time, in January 2003, and cost a paltry €4 million for 120 metres of stainless steel love. And you can't even climb it to admire the view. And the lights don't work half the time.

These gadflies and gossips are quick to forget Ireland's grand heritage. The Spike is, in fact, a fitting monument to the golden (or iron pyrite) age of Irish space travel, and is on the site of a failed moon launch involving an earlier erection, Nelson's Pillar. However, the most famous phallic icon of this ancient era is the Wellington obelisk in Dublin's Phoenix Park. Most Dubliners lazily assume that the 62.5 metre granite pinnacle is a fitting tribute to the Wellington Boot, a remarkable apparatus worn by the common country folk, or occasionally by the Taoiseach when he attends the mysterious National Ploughing Championships somewhere down the Country. They are heathens, they are stupid and incorrect: this big stone hunk of wonder was a prototype military transport, built during a bout of national paranoia over the prospect of a post-Napoleonic attack from the upper atmosphere by the rubber boot's inventor himself, test pilot Arthur Wellesley, Duke of Wellington, Governor of Mysore Arse, aka the 'Iron Duke', who was one of Ireland's first astronauts (or spásaire), although this did not, apparently, make him a horse.

Although construction commenced in 1817, this sweet spacecraft (beautifully adorned with battle scenes cast from captured French absinthe spoons and garlic crushers) was not completed until 1861, some nine years after the Duke's untimely death (naked, in a ham-filled hot air balloon basket). Following a week of trials, the obelisk was deemed too heavy to catapult beyond gravity's reach. It's still there, feel free to kick the tyres and break the windows.

The next notable entry into the Hibernian Space Race was Michael 'The Big Fella' Collins (1890-1922), hyper-immortalized by Ballymena-man Liam Neeson in a magic lantern theatre moving picture show. Collins (a Corkman by all accounts) was one of the blackguards behind the events leading to the formation of the Irish Free State of 1921, and the litany of gorsoonery we've had to put up with ever since. He subsequently served as Commander-in-Chief of the Irish Army, with responsibility for claiming deafness. Thanks to negotiations between El Presidente Éamon de Valera and NASA (National Association for Shy Astronauts), Michael Collins was the first *real* full-blooded Irishman in space without the use of narcotics. He remained in lunar orbit while his Apollo 11 colleagues Buzz O'Aldrin (Mayo) and Nell Armstrong (Antrim) played a hurling match on the moon, thus claiming it for the Gaelic Athletic Association. Some commentators reckon that Collins didn't survive the re-entry impact into the Pacific Ocean on 24 July 1969 after forty-eight years in space, while others claim, with some futility, that he died following an unpleasant acid trip at Béal na mBláth (the Gob of Flowers), near Bandon, West Cork in the same year. These discrepancies have led to suggestions from yet another shower of pundits that the Irish moon-landings were hoaxed by Sinn Féin in a border farmyard in County Cavan in order to bolster the sagging flesh of Irish nationalism: subject matter for a forthcoming tribunal in Dublin Castle.

This magical age of Irish Astronautism was to have an accursed fate, when Nelson's Pillar (illuminated by a Professor Gluckman in 1849, when men were men and electricians were professors and didn't go on strike about light bulbs) met its eruptive end in 1966, in a tragedy compared by the Dalai Lama to the 1986 Challenger Shuttle incident. The Pillar's exit from the centre stage of Dublin's skyward-looking lifestyle is a far from simple matter, however. Several dissident astronautical societies have alternately claimed and denied the notoriety of having done away with it on the fiftieth anniversary of the 1916 Easter Rising, an event that featured the aforementioned Cork seer, astronaut and soldier Michael Collins performing his extraordinary powers of levitation and egg-laying for a waving, cheering and drunk populace, outside the General Post Office on O'Connell Street.

When resting from his endeavours, Collins found time to frequent O'Heffner and Synge's Playboy Club of Western Europe, a late-night wine bar in the basement of the poet Speranza's house in Lower Leeson Street. It was here that Collin's mistress Lady Hazel Lavery, his fiancé Kitty Kiernan and a rabbitskin-clad moon-girl called Chango were introduced to the Irish Space Society by the Count O'Heffner. Chango later became one of the first Moon Collinists, Kiernan went on to play Julia Roberts in *Would Ye Look at Yer Woman*, while Lady Lavery came to a sticky end, in an incident that involved a hot air balloon basket and a quantity of jam.

In today's decadent Celtic Tiger economy, Ireland's contribution to space exploration and extraterrestrial humour is more subtle, with technological involvement in various projects, most notably the European Spaced Agency and the Dublin Institute for Advanced Studies School of 'Comic Physics'. The Institute was once lauded by his holiness Sir Myles na gCopaleen (the son) for having proved, through the talents of Erwin 'The Cat' Schrödinger, that there were two St Patricks and no God.

A new batch of space cadets will soon be recruited. All applications should be forwarded to the Minister for Transport.

Dave Walsh

MOST OF THE INTERNET IS ABOUT BOBBY DARIN

Our research shows that most of the internet consists of Bobby Darin websites.

Imagine our surprise when we ventured to find out exactly what the internet consists of, and we discovered that even the millions of porn sites add up to a relatively minor outpost of the net, compared to the number of Bobby Darin sites.

As of yet there is no rational explanation. One theory is that the internet was originally developed so that scientists could share information about Bobby Darin.

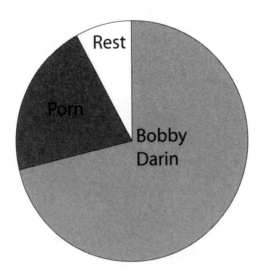

Upon his death in 1973, Darin's body was donated to the UCLA Medical Center for research purposes. The need for international dialogue between scientists may have gained impetus from this, leading to the development of the internet. However, a spokesman for Bobby Darin has insisted that 'scientists have only ever discussed Bobby's singing career' and that his cadaver cannot possibly justify literally billions of websites.

Barry Kavanagh

IRA ANNOUNCES MASSIVE
REDUNDANCIES

(From the archives: a story that first broke on Blather News®)

Outsourcing, globalization and increased cost of knee-capping blamed by regional IRA commanders. 'A disaster for the community,' says murky, balaclava-wearing figure.

(BELFAST) The IRA today announced several hundred lay-offs, effective from tomorrow morning 9a.m. The shocking move comes at the end of a period of intense market speculation, which has focused on the organization's ability to compete in the new 'global terrorism market'.

The economy of the European Union has been in a period of transition: with the inclusion of the ten new member states, the axis of power has shifted. The associated economic impact has been felt globally and, at a local level, made it increasingly more and more difficult for the Army to makes ends meet. 'We simply can't compete', said an IRA spokesman, yesterday. 'The cost of doing business [pushes glasses up nose] is becoming prohibitive in Ireland now. The market has been flooded by cheap Eastern-European labour. These guys will do four times the work at one quarter of the going market rate.'

Knee-cappings, racketeering, maiming, intimidation and battering drug-dealers senseless have always been the portfolio of a home-grown workforce, but now former Eastern bloc countries are offering an abundance of experienced, talented terrorists who will do the same job for a fraction of the price.

Add to this the salient (and all too-often overlooked) fact that there is a small army of scum-bags south of the border willing to off your mother for the price of a Ryanair flight to Alicante, and you can begin to appreciate the situation. Market erosion had been a steady and ever-present factor on the business landscape since the mid-1980s, but now we find ourselves under siege.

said a large, tattooed man that we met in a Belfast car-park.

And it's not just the Republicans who have had to make cuts. High-labour costs and strictly enforced union rules have meant that the UDA have been forced to make radical changes to their employment structures. 'Basically, these Polack lads will come in, hack an arm off, kick a head in, shit on you and throw you in a bog for roughly one third of the cost that one of our lads will do it for. We can't compete against that. We just can't,' said another random man.

'Throw in the fact that they have some serious muscle behind them and well, I dunno. Let's just say that things don't look good for us right now…' he informed us with leaden solemnity. Looking forward, it's hard to see how paramilitary organizations will cope. In the wake of this news, it has been suggested by several prominent economic observers and cross-border Government shit-tanks that the only solution may be a drastic one: make all staff immediately redundant and re-register the organizations in an entirely different country, where management can take advantage of a more favourable tax regime and the cheaper cost of labour. Like Colombia.

Damien DeBarra

THAT WHOLE FATHER PAT NOISE PHENOMENON ON DUBLIN'S O'CONNELL BRIDGE

Having lately returned from the tropics, it took me some time to re-engage with the political hoo-hahs and media blurtings for which our fair isle is well-known. However, I do see it as my duty to stay abreast of issues that concern the plain people of Dublin, like lap-dancing clubs and 'morr-guages', which I'm told is a novel method of purchasing property on the 'never-never'.

After making a landfall at the Pigeon House, I was handed a rolled-up copy of *The Sunday Turbine*. Inside, some hack was wittering on about the 'sudden' appearance of a plaque on Carlisle Bridge (also nicknamed 'O'Connell Bridge'), dedicated to the demise of a Father Pat Noise, who was an adviser to the one and only Peadar 'Knees' Clancy. Father Noise, according to the plaque, died in suspicious circumstances when his coach and four horses plunged hundreds of feet into the abyssal torrents of the River Liffey, on 10 August 1919. Suspicious indeed: his death has apparently been linked by a few snide busybodies to the rise of decadent Cabaret and the signing of the constitution of Germany's Weimar Republic, an event which occurred on the following day.

As people of my generation can attest, 1919 was a very cold summer; we had none of your new-fangled 'global warming' back then, I can tell you. It seems that the steel-clad wheels of Father Noise's carriage slipped on some black ice as he rounded a bend onto the quays. The Holy Father was being pursued by some swarthy gentlemen from a certain law-upholding establishment in Lad Lane at the time, who apparently were aggrieved over Father Noise's alleged failure to cough up a sum of money equal to the pleasure he had experienced in a nearby salon of great discretion. Which is, of course, complete lies: his worship was never shy with flashing a few bob, either at the ladies or the horses.

The driver of the late Father's carriage, hellbent on making for the M4 carriageway, swerved to avoid creasing an aged gentleman who was loitering on Bachelor's Walk, looking for love. The ice (quite thick, even for August) caused the wheels to slide sideways, taking the coach, horses, driver and the late Father through a large hole in the river ice, and into the swirling maelstrom of Anna Livia. A passing itinerant veterinary surgeon and former swimming champion managed to rescue the four horses. The driver was swept away, atop the carriage, but was later rescued near Rockall, where he had been living on a diet of red leather upholstery and fish. Alas, not a trace was found of Father Noise. Some speculate that he later reappeared in public life as Oliver St John Gogarty, who was required to employ several versions of himself in order to uphold his polymathic status. Recent opinion polls suggest that Father Noise is widely believed to have faked his own death, scoring higher than Andy Kaufman, Elvis Presley, Jim Morrison, Ian Curtis, James Dean, Bruce Lee, Jimi Hendrix and Michael McDowell in likely death-fakery.

Now I hear tell that the rapscallions running Dublin City Council want to remove the blessed plaque, claiming that it has only been in place since 2004. This is, of course, so much balderdash, as I was there myself for its installation, during an unseasonably hot December 1920. Based on this claim, the Council plan to replace this splendid memorial to a great friend of the profane, and replace it with a plaque dedicated to a 'real' person. Well, I never, in all my born puff.

Adding insult to injury, I now hear that some young turks – 'students' or somesuch – are claiming responsibility for the creation of the Father Noise memorial, and are touting 'video' evidence as proof. Damn, next they'll claim that the Padraig Sheehan memorial on Hawkins Street is a hoax! Pater Noster my eye!

The Count O'Blather

THE TAOIST PROBLEM PAGE

Do you need answers?! Here are letters taken from the problem pages of magazines. They were meant for run-of-the-mill agony aunts, but we showed them to *our own Taoist sage*, who is never wrong!

SHOULD I GIVE MYSELF TO HIM?

I'm still a virgin. In fact, up until now, I've never had a boyfriend – although I'm in love with a lad at work. The snag is, he has a girlfriend. However, she lives miles away, and rarely comes to see him. When she does visit, I have to pretend to be her friend just so that me and this lad can still spend time together. If I'm honest, things have started progressing sexually between us. We tell our mates that we're 'just friends' but, frankly, there's more going on than that. I love this lad and want him to be with me properly. Should I show him how I feel? I think I'd be better for him than his girlfriend.
Kelly, 21 (Taken from *Chat*).

The Sage says: In your life, you will have sex with many unscrupulous opportunists; you may as well start now.

Blather.net comments: The Sage knows well the ancient Taoist teaching! On his deathbed, the philosopher Chuang Tzu asked that his body be left outside on the ground. He was not concerned that wild scavengers would consume him, because if he was buried, worms would eat him just the same.

IS THREE ONE TOO MANY?

I'm a man whose wildest fantasy has just come true. My girlfriend has just told me that her best friend wants a threesome with us. So why am I hesitating? Why do I think it might not be such a good idea? (Taken from *That's Life!*).

The Sage says: The spontaneity has gone; forget it.

Blather.net comments: The Sage is indeed wise! It is said that a good swimmer forgets the water.

Barry Kavanagh

ENTIRE IRISH NATION GATHERS ON BEACH TO FUTILELY SHAKE FISTS AT SELLAFIELD

(From the archives: a story that first broke on Blather News®)

(DUBLIN) The entire population of the Republic of Ireland are due to gather on Dollymount Strand, Clontarf this coming weekend to join in the world's largest demonstration of impotent fist-shaking at a neighbouring nuclear polluter. 'We're gonna tell them British bastards what's feckin' what so we feckin' are,' said a random drunk, who crawled out from under a nearby rock. Campaign manager Gubnait O'Toss says that the demonstration will 'send a power-ful message to British Prime Minister and British Nuclear Fuels (BNFL) that the Irish people are serious about the issues of nuclear waste disposal in the Irish Sea and that they are prepared to take 'serious measures' to make their case heard.

Irish Government ministers were quick to lend support to the campaign, with Minister for the Environment, Dodgy Roach, claiming that the Irish Government has been pursuing a 'vigor-ous campaign' against the nefarious Albionites and their radioac-tive goo-dumping. 'No more' fumed Roach, 'will the Irish sea be the cess-pool where England dumps its radioactive jism. For too long the island of Ireland has been the continental wank-rag of the British Empire.'

Government spokesmen, speaking under terms of strict anonym-ity, indicated that the government is willing to consider further radi-cal action to make itself and the Irish people heard. Amongst some of the more startling suggestions mooted are a mass staring session, formation frowning, synchronized county-by-county grumbling and a nation-wide simultaneous foot-stamping.

Damien DeBarra

IRISHWOMAN DEAFENED
BY TICKING OF HER OWN
BIOLOGICAL CLOCK

(From the archives: an investigative report from Blather News®)

(GALWAY) Long-term lonely-heart and five-time 'Bunny Boiler of the Year' award-winner Mairead O'Hoop claimed she was struck deaf by the incessant ticking of her own biological clock last night, in the midst of a frenetic round of speed dating. Having successfully scared off five men in under six minutes, O'Hoop (32, possibly 38) was reported to be in the midst of conversing with a handsome manure farmer from Leitrim and was so taken with his manly charms that the passing seconds became akin to the bongs of the Angelus, rendering her incapable of hearing his screams for mercy as she seized him by the genitalia and dragged him to the bathroom.

'We've seen this happen a couple of times now,' said Eimear Grasp, the founder of sweatygropeinthebackofataxi.com, the singles and dating network that facilitates the popular speed dating events of which O'Hoop has been a regular patron. 'Some women, well, they've had about 5,000 dates, are bored to within an inch of their lives and when they actually meet a man who, you know [snorts], they even *suspect* might be a decent skin, they completely lose the plot.' Wailing, screaming, offers of threesomes with sheep and rampant, unchecked coffee consumption are not uncommon in such circumstances.

And it's not just the women, reports Grasp, but indeed the menfolk who have been known to lose the run of themselves at such events. 'One bloke, about two weeks ago, threatened to hack his own legs off with a scythe if a woman didn't give him her phone number. Another shaved all the hair off his back, fashioned a rudimentary noose out of it and threatened to hang himself from the lamppost outside a woman's place of work if a she didn't have coffee with him.'

And it appears that in some instances it's the males who are the worst menaces. 'The worst case we had was the fifty-five-year-old taxi driver who started buying James Blunt albums and learning off the songs in order to woo a sixty-five-year-old Donegal widow. Thankfully the authorities intervened and had him committed before he could hurt himself or anyone else.'

Damien DeBarra

HOW TO FLY A BUILDING

Have you vague feelings that you are searching for something inexpressible? At last at Blather.net we have discovered what you should be doing with yourself. You need to fly a building. Here is our how-to guide.

STEP 1: FIND A BUILDING.

You need to go where buildings can be found. A journey through the heated desert wastes, or the cold snowy wastes, are a waste of time. Also avoid those excessive stretches of lush countryside. Buildings can be found in great abundance in towns and cities, so that's where you should go.

STEP 2. GAIN ENTRY TO THE BUILDING.

Buildings are often surrounded by fences. Obtain a pair of wire-clippers to create a hole big enough for you to get through. Once ensconced in the grounds, wait until a door or a window is opened. Be careful to avoid people who use the building, especially armed security guards. Starting a fire in the grounds can be a wonderful diversionary tactic if you feel that there are too many people concerned with who goes in or out of the building.

STEP 3: LIVE IN THE BUILDING.

Once you have successfully gained entry to the building, it is advisable not to take unnecessary risks by leaving the building, thus necessitating repeated entries, which would require an exhaustive and exhausting amount of stealth and luck. It is best to live in the building for a while. Basements and boiler rooms are rarely visited, and it is here in some bare concrete alcove you should nest. Examine the engine room, to discover the inner workings of the building. This knowledge could be useful later if the building malfunctions during flight.

STEP 4: ASCEND THROUGH THE BUILDING.

Eventually you will have to choose your moment, and use the elevator, escalator or stairs to get to the upper floors of the building. Success in this matter entirely depends on how much the building is in use by other people. Dress so that you are not worth looking at.

STEP 5: FIND THE CONTROL ROOM.

You will find a room in the uppermost or next-to-uppermost floor that has windows all around it. This will certainly be the control room, because a good view of the surrounding area is vital for take-off and landing.

STEP 6: PULL THE BLUE LEVER.

In the control room you should find a blue lever held at a forty-five degree angle. Pull this towards you as hard as you can until the lever is upright. This will disconnect the building from its foundations and allow it to rise vertically into the air. Turn the lever to steer. Observe the height of other structures around you. Avoid crashing into these. Once you have raised the building high enough, fly where you will. Have a picnic in the sky.

Barry Kavanagh

IRELAND'S GREATEST WITS

In October 2007, the lion's share of British media outlets ran with the story that a recent poll, conducted to figure out who was Britain's greatest wit, placed the writer Oscar Wilde at the top of a list of ten auspicious names. And indeed he was a funny chap. There's a slight issue though: Oscar Wilde was not British. Oscar Wilde was (drumroll) *Irish*.

Now we understand that there may be some confusion surrounding precisely what 'Ireland' is. So, in order to help our geographically-challenged cousins in the UK, we suggest that you grab yourself a map of Britain and Ireland. You ready? Good. Take a look (don't rush yourself now, it's not a test) and when you feel good and prepared take a look at that blob on the left. You see that? That's Ireland. Irelaaaaaaand. Where Irish people live. Still with us? Great.

Now you see that big shape on the right? That's Britain. Britaaaaaaaain. Where British people live. That's right: they're two separate countries. For sure, you chaps in Britain own that bit in the north of Ireland (go ask your Mum and Dad) but the bit down south? Yep, that's a separate country. Has been since 1922. No, seriously like. Stop laughing. It's called (you might want to write this down) 'The Republic of Ireland'. It has its own flag and anthem and all. Hell, they even speak a different language in parts of it. It doesn't have the Queen on its money. It doesn't have (shock! horror!) royalty at all.

But no matter; let's not get hung up on semantics. Ah sure, what's a small misunderstanding about nationality between friends, eh? So, in the interest of furthering Anglo-Irish relations, and generally educating the great unwashed, Blather.net now humbly submits its list of *Ireland's* greatest wits for your perusal and comment. Here it is:

10. J. K. Rowling. Widely lauded for allegedly helping fat kids read more books and spend even more time indoors, Rowling has been called 'Ireland's greatest living chancer'. Laugh? We nearly shat ourselves.

9. Emily Brontë. Manically-depressed graveyard worrier from Fermoy, County Cork. Her epic work *Wuthering Heights*, charting the adventures of a roving potato-salesman during the Great Famine, is a real barrel of laughs.

8. Spike Milligan. It says 'I told you I was ill' on his gravestone. In Irish. Also had an Irish passport. Therefore, was Irish. Q. E. D.

7. Charles Darwin. Born 1 April 1815, Clontarf, Dublin. Best-selling 'Limerick' and bawdy ale-tavern songwriter. Winner of 'Greatest Irish Beard' award 1845-49.

6. Banksy. Wexford-born satirical graffiti artist, known for his famous artworks spray-painted over the vomit stains of visiting English hen nights in Dublin's Temple Bar and now sold for up to a million quid to Soho-dwelling tossers with angular glasses and coiffed hair.

5. Ben Elton. Gobby, machine-gun mouthed satirist from Nobber, County Meath. Enjoyed success in the '80s when he co-wrote the groundbreaking RTE show *Blackadder*, following four generations of a scheming Cork family, but now pens musicals re-hashing the back catalogue of Galway rock band Queen.

4. Charles Dickens. Belfast-born Dickens combined vibrant characterization, uproarious dialogue and a healthy dose of the clap to chronicle the daily lives of Mullingar's late nineteenth-century pornographers.

3. J.R.R. Tolkien. Born in Donegal, Tolkien's career as a Trinity College Dublin professor was coupled with a strong desire to re-write what he saw as the 'lost mythology' of Ireland. His opus, *The Lord of the Rings*, addresses this directly, with its 8,000 page chronicle of a Belfast midget's journey to Scotland and back.

2. Salman Rushdie. As Irish as Kenneth Branagh.

1. William Shakespeare. Cavan-born playwright and poet, widely recognized as the world's greatest literary genius. His masterwork *Hamlet* charts the rise and fall of a Cork footballer and his titanic struggle to come to terms with ending up as Sunderland manager, working for a six-foot chicken.

We realize of course that our list might upset some folks, as all such lists are prone to do. Please feel free to submit your own suggestions at Blather.net.

Damien DeBarra

EPILOGUE: THUNDERING MYELOMA

WE BEGIN AS WE BEGAN. SATURDAY 3 JUNE 2006. 6.12PM.

The road to Ennistymon is so Irish you could bottle it and sell it. Twists, turns, grass and dolmens. Hills winding every which way. As the car launches us into another in a series of wild, juddering bounces, myself and Blather.net's chief discuss pressing matters.

'Did I tell you that I modularized the front page now?' he says excitedly.

'Really,' I say levelly.

'It means that if I make a change in one place, that change takes place on every page. Very handy for the individual pages. No more arsing around with html. It all gets a bit messy. I have my reservations about div tags but I think I know what I'm doing now.'

'Uh huh.'

We exchange that look, the one that lets him know I haven't understood a word of what he's said.

'Never mind.'

We briefly discuss the idea of taking acid and sitting on a Dolmen. Instead we stop and have an ice cream. Later, we're pulled in beside a graveyard, seventh-century. The chief consults the map, looking for Sue's house. 'Two miles,' says the chief, putting her into gear and pulling away.

'So which fish is it that I can't eat?' I ask by way of conversation, great streaks of ice cream dribbling all over my hands. He pauses, grimacing slightly.

'Cod,' he says sternly.

'Really?'

'Cod are fucked. Totally over-fished.'

'Jesus. What about tuna?'

'Fucked.'

'Salmon?'

'Totally fucked.'

'Prawns? Don't tell me I can't eat prawns. I love prawns.'

'Prawns are one of the worst problems. Prawns and shrimp have the worst bi-catch rate. That's the amount of other fish that get dragged up in the net with them. For every kilo of prawns caught, harvested and sold as much as ten kilos of other shit gets killed. But even with all that the prawns are still...' he pauses, waving his hand around, the car taking a momentary westward lunge towards a sixth-century BC ring-fort.

'What's the word I'm looking for?' he asks.

'Fucked?'

'Yeah. Fucked.'

TWENTY-FOUR HOURS EARLIER

I'm in Stansted airport. Leaving London. And I'm in Ryanair hell. At any moment I expect a hairy, cloven-hoofed agent of Satan to approach me and try to sell me some aftershave.

'Scratch card?' asks the minion of the dark prince from behind me.

'No thanks. But here's what I would like. I'd like to be on that plane. The one I paid you to be on four hours ago. The one I've been sitting here waiting for. Me and the other 120 people.

The hairy one shifts slightly. 'Train ticket?'

'No thanks,' I say, brushing some flakes of sulphur from my collar. She goes off to speak to another haggard passenger: a big beered-up Irish guy. He looks even more drunk and grumpy than me. He's one of a bar full, sat in Wetherspoons in the darkened airport terminal. Drunk, grouchy, laughing, joking. It's the last saloon in Stansted terminal and delayed passengers are trading Ryanair war stories. Some are angry. Some are more stoical.

'Ah sure lookit. Complaining about the service on Ryanair is like going swimming and complaining that the water is blue,' says a grizzled veteran, slapping a gin and tonic on the table. 'Gimme a light,' he says. I look at him as I hand him the lighter. He knows what he's talking about: a man of fifty-odd, crumpled but expensive suit, lots of air miles. Seen the raw combat conditions of the budget airline business. He, like I, has sat sulking and cursing himself for being a cheap bastard and flying with this shower. He has been sat, disconsolate and in need of a shave, in airport after airport. Alone with nothing better to do than chug down another over-priced, lukewarm beverage, stare at a random woman's arse, and pray to anything that is listening to change the departures board.

It changes. Flight boarding. I make the gate in about five minutes flat. One minor incident with a fascist cabin-crew member later (who seemed to think that my mp3 player could cause serious problems for the aircraft) and I'm in Dublin. Taxi. Wallop. Bang. Keys, sandwich, glass of milk. Blessed, sacred and holy fuck I need some sleep. Lying in bed, I wonder how it is that something I can buy in Dixons apparently has the ability to interfere with the navigation systems of a brand new Boeing 737-800. I wonder am I the only one that finds that unsettling.

THUNDERING MYELOMA

Breakfast. I sit with my Dad in the kitchen. We talk about the latest hospital visit. It looks good. It's been three months now since he matter-of-factly told me has a cancer. Myeloma, to give the malignant little bastard its proper name. To be honest, it seems to be one of those things they didn't even have a name for ten years ago. I've been learning that the word 'cancer' is, in fact, a rather broad umbrella term. We sit, slurping out of coffee mugs, discussing how he is.

'Myeloma,' I say, trying the word out. It feels wrong in my mouth.

'No big deal,' says the father. 'For now,' he adds. He's not in any pain. They're monitoring him closely and he's changed his diet completely. In his favour he's never drank or smoked. They're gonna put him on pills and test him every month. He's as calm as always.

He fills me in on some of the things they've told him at the hospital. On a scale of one to one hundred, he is a fifteen. When it gets to about twenty-five or thirty, they start taking it seriously. That means chemo. But for now, he's fine. He says that his condition is called 'smouldering myeloma'. Unfortunately, whilst he was sitting on a trolley in the hospital, the flap of the double-doors sending a gust up the arse of his gown, the Chinese doctor made a mistake and told him that he had 'thundering myeloma'. We laugh like horses.

Not long after, he disappears out the door and down to the church, where he's involved in helping out with the community. But before he does, we talk about some issues that have arisen at my job recently. I had forgotten that at one stage my father was managing literally hundreds of men, whilst he chased scumbag embezzling union bosses. He spent most of his professional life uncovering corporate fraud. At the same time he was raising five kids, paying a mortgage and dealing with mental illness. He knows how to deal with difficult people and situations at work. I listen. And maybe for the first time in my life, actually hear him.

TEMPORAL BLOG-ANOMALY. SUNDAY 4 JUNE 2006. 11.15PM

I'm drunk. Very drunk. With a pain in my face from laughing. I stand at the door of a pub in Ennistymon, cursing all and sundry that I have to stand outside and smoke. Although I actually came outside because the missus rang. She found the hiccupping amusing. Music is blasting from inside the pub. Locals, bodhrans, guitars and pipes yelping and yowling, elderly couples flinging themselves around.

I hiccup. Squeeze out a sneaky fart. Snigger to myself.

'Bout ye?' roars the chief as I walk back in. He hands me a fresh one. People are slobbering into pints. We're not quite sure what happened earlier, but there was a ferocious ruckus when somebody was borne on a wave of screaming and cheering into the back bar holding a silver cup. Guessing by the decor, we reckon someone's madra has just won a race. There are pictures of whippet-skinny dogs all over the walls. There's been kamikaze drinking.

'Is it just me...' I begin.

The chief grunts into his pint.

'Or is that clock running backwards? The one over the bog door.'

He considers it, lowering the glass.

'It fucking is,' says the chief. It's that stage of the night when he's started, as a result of several gallons of stout and three fat ones, to look slightly edgy. He's giving it the crazy eyes. 'It's backwards alright. Highly-localized, temporal anomaly. Probably caused by the stress-energy from the large gang of elderly men furtively smoking behind that door.'

'What?' Sue asks. She's just been singing and battering the shit out of a bodhran in the middle of a great heaving sea of dancing, porter-guzzling flesh. She sits down, a wine glass swishing about.

'The clock over the toilet runs backwards,' says the chief, fingering his photo lens. She looks over the door.

'Bugger. I thought we had another hour till last orders.'

We drink. We drink some more. There's a brief discussion about the recent societal acceptance of the word 'cunt' and we ask ourselves if there are any taboo words left. Following on from that we discuss a proposal to create a fake news piece which tells the story of how an angry Irish blogger had won a prestigious award for 'most gratuitous use of the word cunt in a single blog entry'. I have no recollection of getting back to the house. I sleep next to a drum kit and a cat. During the night a bass guitar falls on me emitting a long, dull C-flat.

COME HERE OFTEN?

When the sun comes up, I'm out the back door: to look at the birds, sniff the air and watch the light pour over the top of the hill and onto the lake. It's going to be a scorching hot day. Three cows stand some twenty yards away, chewing contentedly. I walk over. One of them, a big white one, stops chewing and stares at me. The second one (a big fresian) stops chewing and stares at me. The third glances at me briefly and continues chewing.

'Morning folks,' I say.

'Morning,' says the white one. The fresian farts.

'Nice day,' I say.

'Lovely,' says the cow.

'Come here much?' I ask.

'Meh,' says the cow lazily, 'not that often. Good in this weather though. Great grass.'

'Yeah. It looks good.'

'You?'

'No. Just here for the weekend. Back to London tonight.'

'Ah, London. Playground of my youth.'

'Yeah?'

'Yeah. I lived in Russell Square. Used to drink with Peter O'Toole. Nice chap.'

'Cool.'

'Yep. That it was.'

We chat: the nearest dolmen, an Iron Age hoard buried in that lake, Wayne Rooney's metatarsal.

'So what has you out here so early?' the cow asks.

'Myeloma.'

'Smouldering or thundering?'

'Smouldering.'

The cow nods. Eventually, I look at the sun coming over the top again. Further now.

'Anyway, I better go. Gotta catch a train. Then a bus.'

'Yeah?'

'Then a taxi and a plane. Followed by a bus and a walk.'

'Well, take it easy man.'
'You too.'
'Seeya.'
'Seeya.'

Damien DeBarra

CONTRIBUTORS' BIOGRAPHIES

Dave Walsh hails from Wexford, where he spent his childhood privateering and wrecking on the river Slaney. He was forced to leave in 1627 after he and an accomplice, William Lamport, were implicated in public horseplay involving a wealthy dowager and an undisclosed quantity of strawberry jam in the Bullring, Wexford. Lamport landed a job in Mexico as El Zorro, but Walsh remained on the run for some time, before changing to a bicycle. Apocryphal reports allude to Walsh keeping a harem of velocipedes in the master bedroom of his Dublin mansion. In 1803, Walsh had a brief epiphany while convalescing from duelling wounds on the Greek island of Corfu. This led to Walsh working for the well-known environmental group Greenpeace, and he now spends his days hand-publishing inflammatory pamphlets from a ship's cabin in the Antarctic, through an ingenious system using steam-driven albatrosses. When he's not raising merry hell on the ocean waves, Walsh can be found imbibing stout in a questionable Dublin hostelry with his pet kakapo, smuggling absinthe from Brunei to Caherciveen, or making scandalous pornographic daguerreotypes of well-known political figures. He has a strange obsession with the Eurasian otter (*lutra lutra*), which as of yet, is not illegal.

Barry Kavanagh was born in Dublin, Ireland, in 1739. He received a degree in English and philosophy from the old University College, Dublin in 1760, but was barred from further studies in natural philosophy because of his alchemical research into the elixir of life.

During the 1760s he circumnavigated the globe aboard the *Dolphin*, the ship commanded by Foul-Weather Jack (the poet Byron's grandfather), and upon its return to Britain he was responsible for the tales of encounters with Patagonian giants that appeared in the *Gentleman's Magazine* and *The London Chronicle*. He worked for the celebrated 'electric medicine man' James Graham in the 1770s, then spent several decades pretending to work as an agent provocateur for and against various European powers and revolutionary organizations. This latter activity – whatever it was – mysteriously culminated in French financial support for the British scientist Sir David Brewster. This was in 1816, and upon receiving the money, Brewster immediately invented the kaleidoscope. After overseeing the commercial development of this colourful instrument, Kavanagh became wilfully reclusive, retreating from the public gaze, although until her death in 1865 he was a known protégé of Princess Caraboo, who famously masqueraded as a lower class servant with the unlikely name of Mary Baker. He was a lover of Thérèse Humbert in the 1870s and Cassie Chadwick in the early 1880s. He somehow re-emerged in public in the twenty-first century, singing with the quiet, reflective musical group Dacianos, who have released three CDs and are currently, in their words, working on 'a masterpiece'. Barry lives in a secret Arctic hideout vaguely inside Norway, writes obvious untruths about the country in a blog, www.blather.net/north, and is putting the finishing touches to a novel that is, in his words, 'like Blather.net except with real people'.

Damien DeBarra was born in 1975 and grew up in Clontarf, north Dublin, Ireland. Having insulted just about every man, woman and child in Ireland and Britain, he decided to chuck it all in and leg it somewhere warm. He then spent a year and a half going slowly mad in Valencia, Spain. After a terrifying experience in an illegal Valencian all-night kebab shop and nightclub (involving hallucinogenic drugs, dehydration and a woman in an Elvis suit) he scarpered to the UK and now lives in London, England. He doesn't talk to anyone and passes the time smiling at people on the tube. He now works in the